BULLS MAKE MONEY

Investment Wisdom
That Stands
the Test of Time

BEARS MAKE MONEY

PIGS GET SLAUGHTERED

ANTHONY M. GALLEA

NYIF

NEW YORK INSTITUTE OF FINANCE

NEW YORK • TORONTO • SYDNEY • TOKYO • SINGAPORE

Library of Congress Cataloging-in-Publication Data

Gallea, Anthony.
  Bulls make money, bears make money, pigs get slaughtered: Wall Street wisdom that
stands the test of time / Anthony M. Gallea.
      p. cm.
  Includes index.
  ISBN 0-7352-0145-5
      1. Investments. I. Title.

  HG4521 .G1835 2002
  332.6--dc21   2001052315

Associate Publisher: *Ellen Schneid Coleman*
Production Editor: *Sharon L. Gonzalez*
Interior Design: *Shelly A. Carlucci*

Printed in the United States of America

10 9 8 7 6 5 4 3 2 1

ISBN 0-7352-0145-5

 NEW YORK INSTITUTE OF FINANCE
An Imprint of Prentice Hall Press
Paramus, NJ 07652

http://www.phpress.com

NYIF and NEW YORK INSTITUTE OF FINANCE are trademarks of Executive
Tax Reports, Inc., used under license by Prentice Hall Direct, Inc.

*To my mother,
Jo Gallea,
who believed in me*

CONTENTS

v

ACKNOWLEDGMENTS

I have many people to thank for this book.

First, my wife, Bonnie, provided support and patience and understanding. It's been a great journey together for the past 31 years and this work is part of that journey.

Chris, Shelle, and Lisa, who were just kids when I wrote my first book, have now all moved on to their own lives in that normal progression of family life. From high school and home, they have traveled on to various universities and then into their careers and lives as they pursue their own dreams and aspirations. I couldn't love you more or be more proud of each of you.

To my partners and colleagues on the Gallea Team at Smith Barney go my heartfelt thanks for our relationships, our friendships, and our work together. This has been one of the anchors of my life and I couldn't possibly wish for better partners. To Richard, Paul, Bonnie, Tara, Sue, Marie, Patty, Donna, Suzanne, Karen, and Valerie, I'm very grateful to you all.

To our management team, Jennifer Hartmann and Donna Caufield, my respect and gratitude for your constant help.

To my editor, Ellen Coleman, thank you so much yet again for helping me bring my ideas to the printed page. Ellen, you really are a joy to work with and you make this process almost effortless.

Anyone can love his advisor when things go well. But it is in times of distress that truth emerges. I will never forget the encouraging words and kind smiles from countless clients who always took the time to think of me, even when they had every right to be thinking of themselves. This is something that I have never forgotten and never will. I've tried very hard to be equal to that trust, and I hope the lessons I have learned over my life serving you have made your lives better in return.

INTRODUCTION

The past decade has witnessed an explosion of new investors entering the markets. With that explosion has come a whole new generation unaware of a great deal of market wisdom that has passed before. There has been a lot of blood and money spilled over the past 100 years in the markets, and there are many hard-won lessons that we would all do well to learn. This book attempts to bring many of these market lessons to a new audience of market participants.

As technology revolutionizes the art of investing, more information is available than ever before to more investors than ever before. Market-moving news travels literally at the speed of light to millions of market players and investors. This has clearly leveled the playing field in terms of information.

However, the speed at which this information is disseminated and the almost instantaneous ability of investors to react have changed the investing landscape. There was a time when a thorough analysis of a company's financial statements was accompanied by a thoughtful review of its annual report and other fundamental considerations. This was the accepted way to do things in the analog age, when the slower pace of information dissemination, as well as the higher transaction cost, made buying and selling a slower and more considered activity.

All that has changed, of course, but I am not convinced that additional speed and greater access to information will, in and of themselves, produce better investors. It is the analysis of that information and the decision not to transact that often sets the consummate investor apart from the less skilled.

I am not an advocate of rolling back the revolution. The markets are bigger than any of us and if this is where they are taking us, hurtling into the future, we can either get on the train or stay in the station. And I am not one to stay in the station.

However, I do believe that the investing community has a collective wisdom, and this wisdom has accumulated over the past hundred years—marking the borders of the modern investment era. There are, I believe, certain basic truths about investing and the markets that still hold true and that are worth learning and remembering.

All through 2000 and 2001, as the Internet and technology frenzy unwound, I read story after story about investors whose portfolios took 50, 70, even 90 percent declines. A lot of that pain could have been avoided if only people had learned their lessons before they put down their cash.

Contained in this book are dozens upon dozens of what I believe to be market truths. Some have been around for a very long time; others are of more recent vintage. Reading this book from cover to cover is the best way to approach it. The book is organized around basic themes, but you can actually open to any page and begin reading. No doubt, you will discover reasons for some of the mistakes you made in the past, and I hope you will also learn just why some of the things you did correctly worked out so well.

Once you have completed reading the book, I'd recommend that you read a section each investing day as a gentle reminder of the lessons contained here.

We would all do well not to confuse speed and plenty with market skill. The fact that we have more information or can act more quickly than before will not necessarily make us better investors. It is in the analysis and thoughtful consideration of what we do that our skills are honed.

This book is based on the lessons I've learned in 20 years of participating in the capital markets as a professional investor. To the experienced investor, some of these market truths will seem like old stuff, but I am frequently amazed at how often they are ignored or forgotten as we get caught up in the hurly-burly of each day's events and opportunities.

Every day my investing skill is tested. It is a never-ending source of frustration that no matter how much I have taken these lessons to heart, I still make mistakes and still need reminding.

To the newer participant eager to learn the ways of the markets, I hope that these lessons provide kernels of wisdom that you have not heard (or heard in the same way) before, and that you will be able to use them as you build a sound investing philosophy. Whether you are a professional or novice, I believe that there is something in this book that will save you from a bad situation. There is something here that will give you guidance when guidance is badly needed. This is a book to keep, to read over and over, to use as a constant reminder of how frail we are and how powerful are the market forces arrayed against each of us as we battle for investment profit.

Some of these lessons I learned the hard (and expensive) way. Others I learned inexpensively from reading and listening. I have learned much over 20 years, yet often I feel that I have learned very little. In that sense, I feel that I'm still a student of the art of investing. Unlike a university program with its finite boundaries, the market has no graduation day marking the acquisition of knowledge.

There does come, however, a day when you will feel that maybe, just maybe, you've learned a little bit, you've paid your dues, and you're a better investor than when you began. Your confidence rises, but you have found a way to avoid the hubris and arrogance that knowledge confers. When you reach that point, slowly but surely, you begin to take profits from the markets and your hard work is rewarded.

It is my hope that what I have written here will guide you on your journey and help you reach that day just a little bit quicker. On the way, I think you will find that investing, in the end, is a journey into yourself. It is a quest that tests our courage, our skill, and our powers of thought and reasoning. Ultimately, we find that the key to investing success lies within each of us.

*The two most engaging powers
of an author are to make
new things familiar and
familiar things new.*

Samuel Johnson, lexicographer
(1709–1784)

PROLOGUE

A TRUE TALE OF WOE

This is a true story.

I love the commodity markets. I only trade them for myself (since the risk is high, and it's not what our clients hire us to do). In 1994, I found myself trading coffee futures for my own account. Weather was the crucial issue. Freezing temperatures, you see, are not good for coffee beans. I can't say that it was all luck, but by the time the dust settled I went out and plunked down the cash for a new Mercedes S500-the model with the little German guy in *lederhosen* who jumps out of the glove box to wash the windows. Thus, I learned the value of successful commodity trading.

Fast forward to Spring 2000. I came across an article that said the 11-year cycle in sunspots was about to reach its peak. When that happens, an abnormally cold winter follows. Sunspot activity affects communications and other atmospheric phenomena. It's true. You can go look it up.

When I looked at the last peak in 1989, I found, to my utter delight, that a very cold winter had indeed occurred that year.

Now I mentioned to my partners that I had found something very interesting and that it pointed to putting on a position. As I rattled on about the vagaries of sunspot activity, I noticed my partners exchanging nervous looks.

"Uh, are you sure you got this one right? It sounds kind of, um, flaky," one of them said.

"Well, you know, I think this one is the real thing. It all seems to line up. You see, the peak activity for sunspot . . ."

Since my partners thought that I was crazy, I was even more determined to show them I was right. I tried the idea on my wife (who thought it was bizarre), on my eldest daughter, a Syracuse School of Management senior ("Dad, we don't study stuff like that."), and over lunch with friends employed by a commodity management firm. ("Uh, that's very interesting," they said, exchanging smiles and winks.)

OK. Me against the world. Convinced that cold weather could create opportunity, I decided that there were two ways I could play the idea. The first would be through the purchase of either heating oil or natural gas futures for February delivery. A glance showed that even in July, the price of both had already moved up substantially, so the risk/reward wasn't as strongly in my favor as I had hoped. In the middle of this analysis, I read that the space station was being adversely affected by significant sunspot activity, which merely threw me into a gleeful frenzy.

In my warped mental state, I saw, gleaming in the sun, the frozen orange juice concentrate contract, which trades as a 15,000-pound item on the New York Board of Trade. Languishing at 78 cents a pound, near its lows, it seemed the perfect way to play the idea. Frozen orange juice concentrate! Frozen oranges!

And so I found myself buying options to buy 300,000 pounds of FCOJ at 85 cents per pound, for delivery no later than February 16, 2001. For that privilege, I paid 8 cents per pound ($24,000). You see, the last freeze (a relatively mild and wimpy affair) had pushed the price up from 90 cents to $1.90, so I was looking for a $300,000 profit. I had a 12-to-1 risk/reward in my favor. Much better.

I came skipping home and announced to my perplexed wife that I now controlled 150 tons of frozen orange juice concentrate, which would become very valuable when sunspot activity froze all the oranges in Florida—we would be rich. She said, "Why don't you go change. Dinner will be ready in 10 minutes."

Flash forward to December 2000. FCOJ is trading at 84 cents, and my options have moved up to 9 cents. An Arctic pig rolls into the United States (an Arctic pig being a huge mass of cold Arctic air heading south).

It rolled through the Dakotas (if it rolls through Montana, I learned, it misses Florida). It rolled across the Plains. It hit the South and barreled right into Central Florida. "RECORD LOW TEMPERATURES," the Tampa paper screamed. "BRRRRR!" said another. "ORANGES HIT BY FREEZING CONDITIONS," blared another.

I danced. I sang. I promised each of my kids a DVD player (our youngest daughter, a film major at St. John's, said, "I like it when Dad buys orange juice.") I whistled while I worked and had a kind word for everyone.

When trading opened on Monday, I was right at my screen, waiting for the glorious moment when OJ would surely open up at a king's ransom in price. At 10:15, I had a wild-eyed look and my hair was askew. I peered expectantly into the screen.

The contract opened *down*, not up. Ladies and gentlemen, when you expect a big move up, and the contract opens down, you say things such as "Oh, oh." You feel like Wil E. Coyote running off the edge of the cliff and suddenly realizing that it's 1,000 feet straight down.

And so it was.

When the Freeze Report Survey was finally released by the U.S. Department of Agriculture people on January 22, it showed that only 3 percent of the crop had been affected. Three percent!

Of course, the position went to dust and so did my dancing, whistling, and singing. I well remember when I put on the position, I said to myself, "Now who would be dumb enough to take on that kind of risk by selling me these options for that kind of money?"

And now I knew the answer—someone much smarter than I am.

As you can see, the moral of the story is that you can be 100 percent correct in your analysis and *still* not make any money. Making money in the market is hard, very hard.

By the way, remember that natural gas contract? It went on to double—$24,000 invested there, in a leveraged option play, would have made me . . . oh, never mind. It's too depressing to think about.

But that's not the end of the story. You see, I'm thinking that this cold weather sunspot thing is real and that with a little bit of luck, I can still convert. So, I'm thinking about that coffee trade in 1994 and the fact that it's winter in Brazil in July . . .

And that's why you need to read this book!

ASSET ALLOCATION

A Little Here, a Little There

THE PERFECT PORTFOLIO
NEVER NEEDS A TRADE.

During my entire life in the markets, I've only sought one thing—the perfect portfolio. I would know when I found it, because the perfect portfolio would never need a trade.

In my dreams, my perfect portfolio has perfect balance, perfect asset allocation, and the perfect mixes of longs and shorts and of commodities, stocks, and bonds. It is perfect in every way.

Each and every stock is a long-term, consistent earnings grower, appreciating nicely at 20 percent per year (the perfect portfolio is not a greedy portfolio). I own 30 stocks in 15 or 20 sectors and industries, all humming along nicely (the perfect portfolio does not know recession).

I'm also short a dozen stocks, each of which has been, for decades, a household name, but I have recognized, before anyone else, that they are in long-term decline. Not that I'm a pig, but my shorts are depreciating at a comforting 10 percent per year.

I've got bonds (good ones, too!) and a few commodity positions, playing a long-term shortage in several. A couple of bets on some interesting emerging markets that I've identified as growth candidates, 10 years hence, occupy a corner of the portfolio. Finally, there's a nice 10 percent position on a major country, just emerging from years of recession.

That's my perfect portfolio: nicely balanced, long term in both scope and nature. I never need to buy anything or sell anything. I don't need to adjust, readjust, or bail out of a bad idea. All the new ideas just don't measure up to the ones I have in my perfect portfolio.

I've never found my perfect portfolio, but there isn't a day that goes by that I'm not striving to build it. From time to time, I latch onto a piece here and there. Sometimes, I find myself in a nice, warm place, and it feels like it could be the perfect portfolio.

Alas, reality intrudes. But I know what the ideal is, and I never give up the chase for it.

IN THE LONG RUN,
STOCKS BEAT BONDS.

For most investors, the single biggest decision is how much to put into stocks and how much to put into bonds. Every other decision pales by comparison. It's called asset allocation. To prove my point, let's run a little race.

Historically, in the modern market era (the era since World War I), stocks have earned their owners about 12 percent per year, and bonds have earned about 5½ percent per year.

Let's say you are a stock-picking genius but an asset allocation dunce. And let's say your neighbor, Bob, is a stock-picking dunce but an asset-allocation genius. As a result, Bob's stocks continually trailed the market and earned him only 10 percent per year (about 2 percent per year behind the market). And while Bob was screwing up left and right, you, on the other hand, were at the head of the class. You held the holy grail of investing. You beat the S&P 500 by 25 percent per year and earned yourself a tidy 15 percent per annum in your stock portfolio.

As an asset-allocation dunce, you had two-thirds of your money in bonds and one-third of your money in stocks, so your average annual return was 8.6 percent per year. Bob, on the other hand, had 100 percent of his money in stocks earning a tidy—you guessed it—10 percent per year.

How could this happen? Well, Bob took two minutes each quarter, threw a dart at s*The Wall Street Journal*, and picked his portfolio. Darts being darts, they weren't great stock picking tools, so Bob trailed the S&P. On the other hand, Bob spent the rest of his time perfecting his golf swing and now sports a five handicap.

You slaved over your research for three hours each day and were nearly abandoned by your spouse because of the time you spent on it, and Bob not only beat you at the investing game but, adding insult to injury, took your money on the golf course as well.

The biggest single determinant of your investment returns is your asset allocation decision. Stocks beat bonds over time. It's like keeping your left arm straight. But don't stop here. Read on . . .

BONDS BELONG IN EVERYONE'S PORTFOLIO.

Stocks beat bonds, but the flip side is that in a bad market, bonds beat stocks. Contrary to popular myth, "Thou shalt only own common stocks" was not the commandment that broke off the tablets. I can't imagine Moses buying a semiconductor stock, but I can imagine him loading up on Treasury bills.

Good-quality bonds offer a steady rate of return and, if held to maturity, don't bite you with losses. In bad markets, in down cycles, in times of recession and depression, they are the investment of choice.

In the rush to experience the thrill of common stocks, too many investors ignore the risks they run, so, when the losses hit, they bail and run into cash. Of course, they do so just as the next bull market emerges from the ashes and begins a solar ascent. Meanwhile, the investor who steadied and cushioned her portfolio with a good dose of bonds has the interest earned from the bonds with which to purchase more stocks. What's more, the bond owner can usually sell those bonds to buy stocks if she wishes.

You're not a wimp if you own bonds, no matter what your friends tell you. Some of my best friends are bondholders, and I can assure you that they're wonderful people.

PRESERVING CAPITAL
IS PARAMOUNT!

The first task of the successful investor is to preserve capital. It is not, repeat, *not* to earn a profit. This may seem strange. After all, investing is an activity that has profit as its ultimate goal.

Profitable investment is underpinned by the belief that a reasonably constructed investment discipline, applied over time, will be successful. Most people nod their heads and then focus 100 percent of their efforts on their discipline. They forget that all of the effort is useless if not applied over time. No matter how well constructed, no investment philosophy that puts money at risk has a high probability of success on a small number of trades or over a short period of time.

Mr. Market is in the business of taking your money from you. He is very good at that. He will find any weakness and ruthlessly exploit it. If you know that danger lurks all about, then you act cautiously. If you're walking alone in a deep, dark forest, you don't break branches and sing in a loud voice. You walk quietly, you tiptoe, you listen intently, and if you hear the brush breaking and hooves pounding, you hide. So it is in the market. You need to be absolutely sure that no matter what is thrown at you, no matter how large the herd bearing down on you, that you'll survive the encounter. Generally, this means paying obsessive attention to your risk and constantly whittling it down as profits balloon the risk of your portfolio.

To be successful, you've got to give your strategy enough time to work. You've got to get into the long haul. You've got to protect your capital, because, without capital, you're out of the game.

Preserving your capital isn't just a game. It's the *only* game. "Nothing ventured, nothing gained" has a flip side: "Everything ventured, everything lost."

YOU'RE YOUNGER
THAN YOU THINK.

As life expectancy has increased, financial advice has been slow to pick up the trend. In grandpa and grandma's day, 65 was old. And so, advice about how much money to have in stocks and how much to put at risk took into account that 1950s nuclear-family–era life span.

But 65 isn't what it used to be, so contemporary financial advice needs to be ratcheted up. Today's 65-year-old has a fair chance of living to be 80 or more. When 65 was old, 72 or 73 was the best-case life expectancy. So, today's 65-year-old should get the advice equivalent to a 1950s 58-year-old.

For most people, 30 percent equities at age 70 or 75 is fine. It's enough extra oomph to increase your returns above the bond market, but not so much to blow a hole in the tanker if the market sinks. After all, what 75-year-old wants to go back to work? If you're in your 60s, then 40 to 50 percent in good-quality common stocks is often perfectly acceptable—you really are younger than you think.

Yes, but you ask, "Stocks will eventually go up, so why not invest a larger proportion of your portfolio in them—say, 75, 80, or 90 percent?" Well, perhaps you will be right. In which case, you'll have another 20 or 30 percent additional capital. That's good.

But, if you're wrong, it may be back to the time clock and the alarm clock.

Your choice.

DIVERSIFY,
BUT NOT TOO MUCH.

Everyone who has a thoughtful opinion on diversification comes to the same conclusion: Diversify your assets. The reason is simple. The more diverse your portfolio, the less the risk of disaster. If all of your money is invested in a single stock, your entire financial future lives and dies by that position, and companies are notorious for stumbling and falling, generally at the worst possible time.

Most people would agree with this strategy, but then the question becomes, how much diversification is enough?

Generally speaking, a portfolio of 10 to 30 stocks provides good diversification. This assumes that the stocks vary by industry and sector. A portfolio of 30 stocks made up of 18 technology stocks and 12 assorted others is really a bet on the technology sector, so any fallout in technology will hit that portfolio particularly hard.

Also, it's worth mentioning that the typical large-cap U.S. mutual fund has a high tracking correlation to such big indexes as the S&P 500 and the Dow Jones Industrial Average, because it probably holds anywhere from 100 to 300 large-cap stocks. So, you don't really become more diversified by buying more than one fund.

Remember, too, that diversification comes at a price. The more you diversify, the more your odds of beating the market go down. The reason is simple: Take the concept to the extreme. If you diversified so much that you owned every stock in the S&P 500, you'd own the index. Here, diversification would be replaced by indexing!

At some point, you've crossed the line and further diversification makes little sense. That point lies somewhere beyond 30 individual stocks or more than one large diversified stock fund. And keep in mind that even as you diversify away the risk of one stock cratering your portfolio, you begin to take on the risk of the entire market doing the same.

CONCENTRATE ON THE FOREST,
NOT THE TREES.

It is the big decision, not the small one, that spells the difference between investment success and failure.

For instance, it is much more important to decide whether or not to invest in stocks than to decide what stocks to buy. The right mix between stocks and bonds is more significant than what specific bonds you buy. It is more vital to get the direction of interest rates right than to pick which single A-rated bond to purchase.

People tend to get all wrapped up in small decisions. Whether evaluating their money manager, working on their own investments, or spending endless hours picking a mutual fund, they seem to feel more comfort in making small decisions. It is ironic that this is so, because small decisions have small consequences.

Think about all the effort expended on picking stocks. It is the national pastime. Once you've picked a stock, it may comprise, say, 2 to 10 percent of your portfolio. As soon as you've done that, you go out and find another one to buy and so on. Eventually, you own 20 or 25 different stocks, all carefully selected. The problem here is that you decided to put only 25 percent of your portfolio in stocks. (That decision probably took you all of 30 minutes.)

Let's assume now that every single stock you picked beat the S&P 500 by a factor of 10 percent (and we'll assume the S&P returned 12 percent for the year—historically, its average), and that you averaged 6.5 percent on your bond portfolio. Your total return on your portfolio was 8.2 percent.

Meanwhile, your neighbor Charlie picked the same number of stocks, but (since he doesn't have your talent) every one of them trailed the S&P 500 by 20 percent. But Charlie, who thinks a lot about the big decision, put all of his money into stocks, so his portfolio returned 9.6 percent.

Now, you ask me, was it superior stock selection (the small decisions) or superior asset allocation (the large decision) that made the difference?

And so it goes. Always, always, drive your process to making big decisions. Spend nearly all of your time on asset allocation in terms of the general movement of the stock, bond, commodity, or currency markets. Spend much, much less time on which stock to buy or which bond to buy.

Get the big picture right and the small things take care of themselves. Of course, if you have unlimited time, with no constraints, then you can think about all these decisions. But, in truth, how many of us have that luxury?

BONDS—
Safety First

CLIP
BIG COUPONS.

Bonds, as an investment, are fairly simple. There are three basic things you need to keep in mind: the interest rate, the maturity, and the credit quality of the issuer. There are a few more minor things, but these are the big three.

People buy bonds for the interest bonds pay and because they want to receive their principal back at maturity. In the old days, when bonds were issued in paper form, all the semiannual interest payments were attached to the bond. You took out your scissors, clipped the coupon, and deposited it in your bank account. When interest rates were high, the coupons were for larger amounts; when they were low, the coupons were for smaller amounts. Today, bonds are issued in electronic format, and there are no coupons to clip, but the idea is the same.

So, the question when buying bonds is, what interest rate will you be paid and for how long? How big a coupon do you want to clip? Unlike a share of common stock, a bond, unless it's a convertible or some such thing, has no significant upside. You get your interest and that's that.

Still, you'd like to maximize the return on the bond. That is, you want to maximize the amount of interest you receive, consistent with a high probability of the issuer paying you back on time. Based on that premise, it would seem perfectly natural for people not to buy bonds until the interest rate was compelling. Then, they would buy them for long periods of time.

You'd think so, hmmm? In my experience, the opposite happens. When things start looking a bit dicey for the bond market (typically because of rising inflation, Fed tightening, or currency weakness), interest rates rise. And instead of generally extending maturities and snapping up those great bond yields, people buy short-term bonds in fear that they might miss even higher interest rates.

Of course, when rates plummet, people rush to the door and try to extend new purchases out into the hereafter. I scratch my head whenever I witness that phenomenon, but I am quite sure that it won't change.

Here's my rule of thumb: When single-A corporate bonds are yielding 8 percent, they're good for a seven-year maturity. Every increase in interest rates should push out your purchase maturity. At 9 percent, perhaps you buy eight- or nine-year bonds. At 10 percent, 10-year bonds. Above 10 percent, get into very high quality bonds and think about 12 to 15 years—but such opportunities only come along rarely.

Conversely, if rates fall below 8 percent, then shorten up. At 7 percent, maybe buy five-year bonds. At 6 percent, three years should do it. Below that, walk along CDs, T-bills, commercial paper, and so forth, and wait it out. Not to worry—all of those stocks you bought will probably take you home.

BONDS LEAD,
STOCKS FOLLOW.

At a stock market top, bond prices will usually start falling first. Interest rates are the vanguard of stock prices, bond prices, corporate profits, and the direction of the economy.

High levels of stock prices evidence an economy that has been robust with increasing corporate profits. As the demand for goods increases, inflation tends to firm. The Federal Reserve, ever mindful of its obligation to control that inflation, often tightens interest rates in the hope of slowing the economy, which, of course, means that bond prices go lower.

At stock market bottoms, the opposite occurs. A weak economy, in need of stimulus, causes the Federal Reserve to ease up on interest rates. Bond prices rise, and stock prices tend to do so shortly thereafter.

So, a rise in interest rates can signal a market top, and a decrease can flag a market bottom. Bonds tend to lead stocks at both tops and bottoms.

BE AN OWNER,
NOT A LENDER.

When you purchase a share of common stock, you become an owner in that business—to be sure, a small owner, but an owner nonetheless. Conversely, when you purchase a bond, you become a lender to the issuer. So, if you own 100 shares of Ford Motor, you're an owner, whereas if you buy a Ford Motor bond, you're Ford's lender.

This concept of owner versus lender can help clarify why stocks offer greater appreciation over time. Owning a business has a greater upside potential than lending to one. When you lend, you've got a fixed potential return (the interest rate you are paid), but when you lend money, you risk the entire investment if the company can't pay you back.

As an owner, you have the same risk as the lender (the stock could go to zero), but you have a much greater upside potential. As a matter of fact, I bet you can quickly name a dozen people who've become wealthy as business owners, but you'd need a three-martini lunch to come up with 12 people who became wealthy as lenders.

As you know, your banker tries to borrow money as cheaply as he can and then lend it out at as high a rate as he can. Along the way, some of the loans go sour, and there are long, brutal meetings in the bank about it when this situation gets out of hand.

Be an owner whenever you can.

THERE IS NO SUCH THING
AS A FREE LUNCH.

The fixed-income portion of your bond portfolio should be designed to pay you a market rate of interest without default on the underlying bonds you own.

Now, as your bonds roll over, or as you have new cash to invest, the bond market may not always be ready to accommodate your needs. For instance, if you have a target return of 8 percent for your fixed-income portfolio, and new seven-year investment-quality bonds are yielding 6.8 percent, you may be tempted to stretch for yield to hit the target on your new purchase.

There are two ways to stretch. You can buy a longer-maturity bond, or you can buy a lower–credit-quality bond. Instead of that single-A, seven-year corporate, you stretch to a 10-year, BBB- corporate and congratulate yourself on picking up an 8 percent yield.

In the bond market, as in most everything else, there is no free lunch. If you get eight instead of six-point-something, you're being paid a bit more for taking on additional risk. The risk is a greater chance of either default or rampaging inflation that eats up the value of your interest.

I would suggest that you take the lower risk and settle for six-point-something. Look, if interest rates are low, you should be able to make a lot more money in the stock market, allowing you to hit your overall return numbers.

When interest rates rise, it usually signals a coming inflation or a possible recession if the Fed is engineering a tightening. In that case, higher credit quality is a very good thing to have when economic bad times shake out poor credit risks. And, a rising interest rate environment favors owners of short-term bonds over long-term bond owners.

Stretching for yield isn't a good idea. When you find yourself thinking about doing it, ask yourself if the additional risks inherent in doing so are worth the additional yield you can get.

You'll find that the answer is always the same.

DON'T MORTGAGE
THE FUTURE.

Keep the mortgage portion of your bond portfolio below 35 percent. Mortgages can be great investments in tax-deferred accounts such as IRAs, Keoghs, and pensions. Generally, though, you don't want to buy them outside of tax-deferred accounts, because the tax accounting for repayment of principal can be a real rat's nest. Did you ever try to eat the legs of the lobster? It's a lot of work for very little satisfaction.

At any rate (no pun intended), mortgages offer great current cash flow, typically monthly payment of principal and interest, so you've got more cash to work with to fine-tune and adjust your portfolio. Also, mortgages, because of their uncertain payback schedule, generally carry a higher interest rate than a comparable government or corporate bond. The uncertainty is created because when interest rates make a big move, homeowners will refinance their mortgages, and when they pay off the old ones, you get your principal back much sooner than you anticipated. Given the implied or overt government backing of many mortgage securities, credit quality is high, so that's not a particular worry.

If you load up on mortgages, you may find yourself back in cash when you don't want that to happen.

So, like a little bit of cayenne pepper in your salad, a little bit of mortgage investing can add some interesting zip to your portfolio. You get monthly payments and some of your original investment back each month, which boosts your cash flow. But, like the red stuff, too much can really burn.

Roughly, once your portfolio crosses the 35 percent level for mortgages, the uncertainty of the payback begins to increase the risk of the portfolio.

Here's the other side of the coin: If you have the foresight and wisdom to buy those mortgages when rates are high, you'll find, much to your regret, that when rates plummet, homeowners will refinance and hand you back your money. And, if rates soar, those mortgages won't be paid back a day sooner than they have to be. Meanwhile, their value on your statement drops—a disconcerting fact of life for the mortgage investor.

Now, assuming no credit default, you will certainly get back every penny that you put into the mortgage, so no matter what the value on your statement, it will eventually all come back to you at 100 cents on the dollar.

For most investors, a mortgage portion of, say, 35 percent of your entire fixed income portfolio is about it. It's enough to help yield and current cash flow, but not so much to really zing you if rates go up.

DON'T BUY JUNK.

Buying junk bonds, penny stocks, and fractional out-of-the-money options is, for most investors, to be avoided. Each of these securities is among the poorest values in its respective asset class. Why then do people buy them?

There is a single reason: big payoff. Any one of those investments has the potential for an outsized profit. A junk bond paying 16 percent interest can move up into good credit quality and so create a virtual annuity at well above market interest rates, not to mention an increase in price on the credit upgrade. A 30-cent penny stock could eventually work out into a $30 stock—100 times on your money. And, that nearly worthless option that you paid only $1/16$ for could get struck by takeover lightning and soar to $5.00—80 times the amount invested.

Given those mouth-watering potentials, it's no wonder people fall into these dubious investments.

What they don't understand, of course, are the extremely long odds that they face in this type of activity. And this lack of understanding is completely unnecessary. You might think that people simply can't compute the odds, but they can. And so can you.

Just look at the price. The cheaper the price, the longer the odds.

BULLS AND BEARS—
What Goes Up Must Come Down

SELL INTO A "CORRECTION," BUT BUY THE "BEAR MARKET."

A bear market is generally defined as a 20 percent drop in the major market averages. To be honest, I've never been able to find the original source for this, but the 20 percent rule is one that everyone seems to accept. It is important because the words *bear market* are charged with meaning. Somehow, a "bear market" sounds much more ominous than a "correction." A correction seems almost benign, as in "I misspelled Mississippi, but I put in a correction and now it's OK," or "Stock prices were a bit too high, so we corrected that." Nice and polite, no harm, no foul.

But a "bear market"? Oh my! And so commentators, fearful of the beginning of a bear market, will often say, "We believe a correction is overdue." A correction! We breathe a sigh of relief.

The truth is that bear markets begin with corrections. A correction is the seed of a bear market. And, truth is, no one really knows if a correction is going to stop at 10 percent (another commonly accepted definition) or if it's going to turn into something much worse.

Words are charged with meaning and, to the extent that they worry or comfort, our investment strategy can be hindered by them. When someone says "correction," don't assume that something mild and benign is about to happen. He's saying that a decline in prices is upon us, and that isn't something to take lightly.

Finally, you should also know that the same commentator won't generally call it a bear market until the decline in prices has brought stocks back down to reasonable levels. Put another way, consider selling into the "correction" and buying the "bear market."

THERE ARE NO BULLS OR BEARS
IN A BAD MARKET.

Consider two investors in a bear market (prices having generally been marked down by 20 or 30 percent). One is fully invested and in a lot of pain. The other is sitting in cash, waiting to invest.

You could ask them if they were bullish or bearish. Empty exercise. If you're in a bad market and up to your ears in stocks, you're *hopeful*. You're hoping the market goes back up so you can get out even, and to prove yourself worthy of that happy event, you promise never to overdose in stocks again.

If you have cash, you're opportunistic. You're thinking about what you want to buy and what is going to move first once the turn comes.

Each investor has a market opinion driven more by his emotional state than a rational assessment of stock prices. If your boat is fully loaded with equities, can you say you're bearish?

YOUR BULL MARKET RETURN
WILL BE EATEN UP BY A
BEAR MARKET.

Investors in a bull market often wonder why it pays to be cautious. A simple example will explain it all: A strong market gives you three years of positive, 20 percent per year returns. After 36 months, your portfolio has increased from $100,000 to $160,000 (for simplicity's sake, we'll ignore compounding).

A two-year bear market strikes and lops 20 percent off stock prices (the usual definition of a bear move). Your $160,000 has dropped to $128,000. This means that after five years of investing, you have a total return of 28 percent, about 5.5 percent per year. You would have had about the same return in a money market fund. For the risk you took, you really received very little in the way of incremental return!

Frankly, very few people will sit down with a calculator and do the math. For every one who does, I would bet that there are 1,000 who have endlessly compounded a good year's return to determine their position after 20 years. "Let's see now, if I could make 18 percent a year for the next 19 years, just like I did this year, I'd have . . ."

When you think about potential returns, you must factor in a bear market. Bear markets, despite what you may believe from the returns of the 90s (although some of you may have gotten an education in 2000!), are a fact of market life and will be with us as long as greed and fear need correcting.

Moral: Remember that your bull market return will be clipped by a bear market. Financial planning that does not take this into account is, simply put, bad planning.

BILLS AND BULLS
DON'T MIX.

The Buffalo Bills have their roots firmly planted in the old American Football League. As a long-suffering Bills fan (will we ever win *that* game?), the one thing I've never blamed the Bills for was a bad year in the stock market. I'm referring, of course, to the Super Bowl indicator.

It has been accurate enough. When a team from the original National Football League wins the Super Bowl, the odds overwhelmingly favor a bull market in the current year. When an American League team wins, look for the bear to come out of hibernation.

I've thought a lot about this one. Originally, I thought that because the NFL teams were located in the old rustbelt cities (Detroit, Pittsburgh, Cleveland), only a good economy would juice up the residents and owners in those cities and inspire those teams to catch footballs and leap across the goal line. That would explain it. But there have been so many exceptions to this trend that I doubt this dubious analysis is correct.

What I've come to believe is that it's a neat coincidence but no more than that. It's similar to the fact that Abe Lincoln's secretary was named Kennedy and John Kennedy's was named Lincoln—odd historical quirks that don't really offer a market edge.

I have, however, vowed to keep an eye on the average weight of the Bills' defensive four. My reasoning is that if they can move above 300 pounds each, that might indicate a good year ahead and once again make me a believer in the Super Bowl indicator.

On the other hand, the thought of watching all that beef heaving and pushing all season might take some of the fun out of the equation.

ECONOMISTS HAVE PREDICTED 12 OF THE PAST 7 BEAR MARKETS.

There was an old gag line that Wall Street seers pulled out whenever an economist threatened a bull market with a pessimistic economic forecast. (What! A recession! Damn!) And it was mildly amusing because, like all humor, it was based in reality.

Trained by the Great Depression, economists predicted dire events once World War II was over . . . all those troops returning, all those defense factories without orders. Of course, the downturn never happened. But that didn't keep them from regularly predicting recession/depression all through the 50s, 60s, and 70s.

Charged by the terrible decline in the economy and stocks in the mid-70s, the "dismal scientists" picked up their recession mantra again in the 1980s, but by the late 90s, they had substituted a Barney's suit for sackcloth and ashes. Full of the wonders of the managed central bank economy ("We've learned from our mistakes," huffed one crystal ball gazer), the worm has fitfully turned over.

In recent years, the economic argument is over whether or not recessions have been banned forever. Only curmudgeons and central bankers are left to believe that recession is possible any longer.

All of this leads to one and only one rational conclusion: In the future, economists will predict 12 of the past 7 bull markets.

FOLLOW
THE MONEY.

I've seen this happen several times and it's always the same. Investors, overly pessimistic about the prospects for the stock market, are caught flatfooted when a bull move begins. Whether in 1982 or at the start of the Gulf War, the initial move is always brawny and all-encompassing. Everything seems to move.

Concerned about which stocks will "stick" as the market moves higher, many people sit on the sidelines, wringing their hands and waiting for the reappearance of old lows, which they will not see again. Make it easy on yourself. Buy a big brokerage or financial services stock. If the bull market is for real, the financial services sector will do very well indeed over the life of that market, as business gets better. It's one stock you can put in your core bull market portfolio.

MOST BULL MARKETS HAVE
A COPPER CEILING.

As every veteran trader knows, rising commodity prices are bad for stock prices. Commodities such as copper and oil are essential products. But they're also key ingredients for some of the most important products we buy. In essence, rising copper (or oil) prices mean manufacturing costs rise. When commodity prices rise, it makes sense to assume that two things will happen.

Unable to raise prices in a competitive environment, manufacturers see their profit margins squeezed. As a result, their earnings stall or even fall back. And those higher costs are passed along to consumers in the form of higher prices. That means that consumers actually see a reduction in the amount of money they have available to spend on other things.

Neither is good for stock prices since investors typically want growth, and stagnant earnings mean lower stock prices. Nearly 70 percent of the economy's growth depends on consumer spending, and any cut in spending causes the economy to contract and overall growth to slow. That translates into lower sales and lower profits for companies, resulting in lower stock prices.

When you're in a bull market, look up. Hitting your head on a ceiling—especially a copper one—can be painful. Toward the end of an economic expansion, demand for commodities tends to increase as supply is outstripped. Since copper is used for a wide range of industrial uses, it signals robust demand and increasing commodity prices. This inflationary tendency is then fought by increasing interest rates, so the chain reaction is to lower stock prices as competition from bonds increases.

WATCH
THOSE CURVES!

An inverted curve is a bullish signal for utility and other interest-sensitive stocks. That's because when the Fed tightens up on interest rates, the yield curve will often invert. This simply means that short-term interest rates are higher than longer-term interest rates. As this happens, utilities and other interest-sensitive stocks (bank stocks, for example) fall off in price as the cost of funds rises.

But, even as these equity prices fall, it is a point of interest to the prudent speculator that an inverted yield curve is not a normal one, so depressed prices beckon examination for capital commitment.

I have found that an inverted yield curve often offers an opportunity to buy interest-sensitive stocks at a discount. Inverted curves aren't the norm and should be exploited for opportunity.

NEVER CONFUSE BRAINS
WITH A BULL MARKET.

This is another one of those old Wall Street sayings that's worth repeating endlessly because so many people forget it.

In a good, old, rip-roaring bull market, most stocks go up. And some stocks go up a lot. It's the proverbial rising tide lifting all the boats. Now, if the tide is lifting your boat, you don't yell over to the guy in the next boat, "Hey! Bob! Look at how smart I am. My boat is rising!" You can't take credit for the law of buoyancy. So it is in a bull market. The market goes up and drags just about everything with it. You don't yell, "Hey! Bob! . . ."

It's like this: Everyone wants to be a player. Everyone wants the pleasure of being the stock picker. Everyone wants to beat the S&P 500 and tell the world about it. So you have, maybe, a million investors all owning stocks, and by virtue of the law of buoyancy, a few thousand are going to thrive. They just own the right combination. Somebody's got to own the right combination! And of that few thousand, there may be a few, a very few, who have the right to take credit for what they accomplished.

But it will be hard to find them, because, in my experience, the ones who really deserve the credit will give the credit to the bull market. It's a subtle thing, but it separates the very best from everyone else. You see, the very good will tell you that they're just lucky, and the lucky will tell you that they're very good.

IT'S THE FED, STUPID!

The stage is set for a new bull market when falling interest rates, cash on the sidelines (mutual fund cash and inflows are among the good indicators), good values in the market as indicated through fundamental analysis, and lots of investor pessimism are present.

And the Federal Reserve, through interest rate policy, has a lot to say about the direction of the economy. Generally speaking, when the news is bad and the Fed is easing up on interest rates, it's not a bad time to buy stocks.

BUYING OR SELLING SHORT—

The Game Begins

THE STOCK MARKET FAVORS BUYERS
OVER SELLERS.

It's a fact. You can go look it up. The stock market rises or stands still about 80 percent of the time. That means if you are going to be a short seller, trying to profit from a decline, you've got long odds against you. Most of the time you're going to be wrong.

In a rising market, most stocks go up. The good ones go up and so do the bad ones. The implication is that the first thing you need to do is be right about the market. You've got to be selling short in that 20 percent of the time when the market will help you out. In bad markets, most stocks go down.

Second, you've got to pick an overpriced stock. It's not enough that the underlying business stinks, but you've got to find out that it stinks before the rest of the world has caught onto that fact. If you're wrong about the business, the stock won't go down. If the rest of the world has already figured it out, the stock will already have declined, taking most of your short selling profit potential with it.

You need to find a stock with a bad business before the rest of the world catches on, and you've got to have enough downside in the situation to give you a profit. I would do a back-of-the-envelope calculation and estimate that your odds of successfully selling a stock short are probably one in 20 or one in 30. This is why there are so few short sellers. Many try, and it's a legitimate market activity, but by the time you add up the odds stacked against you (remember that almost everyone else is trying to push stock prices higher), you've got a tough row to hoe.

Almost all investors are better off focusing on the long side. If you think stocks are overpriced, go to cash and take some time off. It'll all be there when you come back. A good vacation is usually a lot cheaper than selling short.

INVEST IN HASTE,
REPENT AT LEISURE.

Good investing requires careful thought, a sound strategic and tactical plan, reasonably thorough analysis, and good judgment. Like any other complex undertaking, investing has a lot of moving parts that have to work together for it to work. For example, you may buy a perfectly good stock, only to have an economic firestorm, such as the Asian currency crisis, pound your position.

Given the great difficulty inherent in successful investment, you need all the time you can spare to apply yourself to the task. This means that the less time you spend thinking about an idea, the more likely that idea is to fail.

People are fooled into believing that because it's easy to get into a position, it doesn't require a lot of thought. They confuse the ease of entry with the work required before entry. Others, in a rush to not miss the proverbial sure thing, jump in without considering the risk, let alone the worthiness of the idea.

Take your time before getting into a position. Think about why you are making the investment, how much to invest, and the reasons why it makes sense to you. Do your research, do your homework. As you explore the various aspects of the idea, you may very well think of a negative that at first glance you missed.

If you invest in haste, more often than not a loss will result. And unlike the speed with which you made your move, you'll have lots and lots of time to regret it.

Buy high;
Sell higher.

There are two kinds of investors: momentum (growth) and value. Either is a legitimate and reasonable approach to investing, but you've got to be sure that your investing style is in harmony with your personality. If you're not sure what kind of investor you are, here's some help:

- When you shop, do you simply buy what you want at the price quoted?

- When ordering in a restaurant, do you tend to look at the price last?

- If you rent a car, do you return it with the gas tank partially empty and pay to have the rental company fill it for you?

- You never clip coupons, right?

If all of these things sound like you, then you're probably a momentum investor. Momentum investors buy high and try to sell higher. They want to own a stock that's already in a definable trend. They don't care if they buy near the bottom. They're happy to pay up for a stock that appears to be a sure winner.

If this describes you, don't worry about picking bottoms. It's just not your style. Instead, find those markets and those investments that suit your personality. If gold has moved from $280 to $350, and your value-oriented friends are clucking their tongues over the "extended move" and admonish you to "worry about a correction," ignore all of that. If you want to own the thing, own it.

But don't forget the second part: Sell higher.

DOUBLE UP
ON WINNERS.

Buy more of a good position. This is a hard one to learn. It's hard because people either don't do it, or if they do, they overdo it.

After you've entered a position, you'd like the market to vindicate your judgment by showing you a profit. When it does that, it's a signal to you that you're on the right track and you might want to take a slightly (slightly!) larger position.

Let's say you buy December Silver at $5.00 per ounce. The market moves up 2 percent to $5.10. Given the 5,000-ounce contract, you've now got a $500 profit. Buy another contract (but don't buy five!). Your average cost is $5.05. Set a stop-loss at $5.05. Your worst case is breakeven. Huzzah! Silver moves to $5.25. You've now got a 20-cent–per-ounce profit ($2,000). Buy a third contract. Your cost is now $5.11. Raise your stop to $5.15. You've locked in a four-cent profit ($1,200). Give the contract room to move without stopping you out.

Now, let's say Silver moves to $5.50. You sell. Fifty cents on 15,000 ounces is a $7,500 profit.

The real world isn't quite this perfect by a long shot, but you get the idea. You enter a position, dipping your toe in the water. When it moves your way, you buy a bit more, but you protect yourself with a stop because you're putting more at risk: a higher price, a little more on the position. You're buying into strength, moving with the trend, riding a winner. That's good trading.

If there's a stock you want to own, and you'd like a position of 2,000 shares, don't buy all 2,000. Buy 500 (stick your toe in the water). If it moves up, buy another 500 (now going in up to your waist). If it moves again, buy another 500 (your chest is covered). Finally, buy the last 500 (gurgle, gurgle).

Yes, I know. Your average cost is higher than if you just bought the 2,000 right out of the gate. But you'd be surprised how many times you stick your toe in the water, swishing it back and forth with your sand pail in your hand. Then, suddenly aware of something different, you sense a lazy twitch of grace and see a large fin knifing silently through the water.

BUY YESTERDAY'S WINNERS.

Be a contrarian. Bill Patalon and I wrote an entire book on this one (book plug: *Contrarian Investing*, published by New York Institute of Finance/Prentice Hall), so I could go on for quite a while on this topic, but let's distill it into a nutshell.

At some turning points, the overwhelming mass of opinion has come to believe that something is true. To determine whether or not there is cause for being a contrarian in any given situation, you must first find out whether or not that opinion is universally held.

Everywhere you go and look, are people uttering the same thing? Let's think about what that means. It stands to reason that if everyone believes something to be true, presumably they've all acted on it. If they've all acted on it, then there isn't any additional pressure to keep the thing moving in the same direction (up or down). And since there isn't additional pressure for the trend to continue, the path of least resistance is in the other direction, since it wouldn't take very much to push things the other way.

Now, if your goal is to buy low and sell high, it stands to reason that you can't buy popular investments. If you buy what's popular, the price has already moved and what you are really doing is buying high and selling higher.

In buying low, you've got to look at what's out of favor and unpopular. You've got to go against conventional wisdom and popular belief, and then you need the patience to wait until events prove you right.

So you start with yesterday's winners. Not yesterday as in yesterday, but yesterday as in history. When you find a big blue chip company in the dumps, when you find opinion almost universally negative, when you find investors have bailed out in droves and now consider the company uninteresting, you should be interested. And when those lovely words "It's dead money!" are uttered, then perhaps you've found a gem in the rough.

Over time, you will not make a lot of money overpaying for stocks, or commodities, or funds. You need to find bargains, and those bargains are in yesterday's winners. There was something that made them winners and, presumably, unless it was something very transitory, those circumstances will occur again, and you want to be there with capital committed *before* that happens.

After a Market Break, Buy What Recovers in Price.

There is nothing quite like a market break to show you where to find the strongest investments. Good investments will recover quickly, and poor ones will stay pinned to the mat. In a market decline, almost everything will decline in price: the good, the bad, and the ugly. Amazingly few stocks are spared the decline, and declines tend to be almost universal, just as roaring bull markets tend to be universally good.

But once the market begins to recover from the decline, the best stocks lead the way, being the first to move. I would guess that this happens because investors, still fearful and wary after a punishing decline, are only willing to step up to those stocks that they feel can stand further decline. They want high-quality, liquid positions with good prospects. Investors, at a market bottom, lack those speculative animal spirits that allow them to pick stocks of questionable virtue—*that* comes later.

After a market decline, when deciding what to buy, look to the upside leaders. You will hesitate because you'd like to get the lower, bottom price of a few days earlier. But, in waiting, you'll miss the easiest profits that are possible at the bottom. Strong stocks are usually the first to rise and the last to fall. Work that to your advantage.

YOU PAY FOR LIQUIDITY, BUT LIQUIDITY IS A SOMETIME THING.

Many investors are aware, at a subconscious level, that one very big reason they are willing to pay sometimes outrageous prices for stocks is their assumption that they can get out when they want. Put another way, they may know that the stock is overvalued, but they assume that they'll be able to unload quickly, at a reasonable price should they need to do so.

It is this illusion of liquidity that can wreak havoc on the unsuspecting. Liquidity exists simply because there is a ready supply of motivated buyers and sellers, all buzzing around the same price levels. It is this high level of buyer/seller interaction that allows for liquidity. Liquidity—the ability to get in or out without a lot of price disruption—exists in those pockets of high-transaction populations.

But, just as moths are attracted to the flame, blowing out the candle can just as easily disperse them. When a storm of good or bad news hits the stock, it throws the relatively evenly balanced buyer/seller motivation out of kilter and results in price disruption. Absent a motivated and roughly equal population of buyers and sellers, price must move to a level where it's once again at equilibrium. That process can leave you breathless.

You need to remember this every time you buy or sell. The liquidity you need may be there today, but there is absolutely no guarantee whatsoever that it will be there when you have to close the position. If investors paid more attention to that, perhaps they would insist on a discount in the price to reflect possible liquidity, and thereby might mitigate some of the disasters we see and, all too often, experience.

ALWAYS RUN
THE NUMBERS.

Generally, high turnover results in lower returns, though this isn't an absolute. Some speculators are able to overcome the drag of turnover, but they are in a very small minority. In general, turnover hurts most investors' returns. A quick look at the math will convince you that this is so.

Turnover creates three types of costs: commission, trading spread, and taxes. Let's take a look at each of these to estimate their drag on a portfolio.

Let's say you've been successfully market timing ABC Widgets. Uncertainty about their new Biotech Widget has created wide trading swings as the news lurches bullish and bearish. You've bought and sold $300,000 worth of ABC in your $100,000 account, for a turnover rate of 300 percent. What kind of returns can you expect and at what cost?

Assuming an average price of $10 per share, you've bought and sold 30,000 shares of stock. This actually means you've traded 60,000 shares: You bought 30,000 shares and sold 30,000 shares. Assuming an average trade of $10,000, you've executed 60 trades in ABC, at an average commission of $8 per trade, or $480 in commission expense.

Next, you've generally had to pay the offering price when you bought, and you received the bid price when you sold. Since ABC is fairly active but extremely volatile, the spread has generally been 10 cents per share: bid $10; offer $10.10.

On 60,000 shares, you've paid about $6,000 in spreads, which means that as soon as you buy at 10.10, the stock has to move up 10 cents (bid 10.10, offer 10.20) for you to break even. So the trading spread cost is $6,000.

Now you've got to deal with Uncle Sam. On every trade you make, he's in for about 40 percent. Since you're swinging away on a short-term taxable basis, each trade gets taxed at ordinary rates.

So, what is our hurdle rate to earn 10 percent on our capital? First, we've got commission costs of $480 and spread costs of $6,000. Just to break even, we need to earn $6,480. Then, in order to pocket $10,000, we need to earn $16,667 in order to get 10 percent, or $10,000, after tax.

Adding this all up,

$16,667	pretax profit to net $10,000
6,000	trading spreads
480	commission costs
$23,147	gross profit needed to net 10 percent after tax

This means you've got to have a gross profit trading return of 23.1 percent just to net 10 percent. We're not even adding in compensation for your labor or costs of newsletters, computers, software, and/or trading programs.

If, instead, you had just bought ABC and held it for 366 days, you'd only need to earn $13,766 (a bit more than half of the preceding total) to get the same percentage gain:

$12,500	pretax profit to net $10,000 (long-term gain tax at 20 percent)
1,250	trading spreads
16	commission costs
$13,766	gross profit needed to net 10 percent after tax

You can see why Warren Buffett likes to buy and hold for long-term gain and why trading is such a tough way to make money. The math is inescapable. It is because the math is so clear that I believe that people who trade aren't really doing it for the money. It may be entertaining, it may be exciting, but if you want to maximize profits, buy and hold.

CREATE A LEVEL
PLAYING FIELD.

One of my favorite models for judging the value of a stock is the PEG ratio. You construct the PEG ratio by dividing the price/earnings multiple of the stock by its growth rate.

Example: Amalgamated Widgets is selling at $20 and will earn $1.00 per share this year. Its earnings have been growing at a rate of 40 percent per year. The P/E multiple of the stock is 20 ($20 divided by $1.00). And the PEG ratio is 0.5 (20 divided by 40). If the stock rises to $80, then the PEG ratio will have increased to 2.0 (80 divided by 40). Note that you don't divide by 0.40, but rather by 40.

When the PEG ratio is less than or around 1.0, then the stock is reasonably valued to its growth rate. As the PEG ratio increases, the valuation becomes more expensive. As a general rule, I don't like to buy stocks whose PEG ratio exceeds 1.0, and when I own a stock and the PEG ratio exceeds 2.0, I consider selling it.

One of the nice things about the PEG ratio is that if you are considering three stocks for purchase, the PEG ratio is a level playing field upon which to evaluate how expensive each stock is.

The bottom line is that you don't generally want to pay more than one times the growth rate of the company, as measured by the PEG ratio.

BUY THE RUMOR;
SELL THE NEWS.

This old Wall Street saw is frequently quoted for a good reason: It's usually true.

As much as we would rather not admit it, the fact of the matter is that news, both good and bad, leaks out into the market. It's not always the case, but it is fair to say that as often as not, an investment will move in anticipation of a news event and the news will prove the move correct. Often, the actual announcement is greeted with a move in the direction opposite the news. ABC Widgets might rise from $22 to $28 without any discernable reason. Then, the company announces a new advanced biowidget that will increase sales by 50 percent (their competitor, XYZ Widgets has no such product) and the stock sells off to $26, leaving those buying the stock on the news stranded.

You see, when people hear some news and then react, they're often too late. The information has been leaking and the market has been sniffing out the truth. By the time it's in your morning paper, the move, or most of the move, has already occurred.

So, it's not so much that you should buy the rumor, because that's generally a good way to lose a lot of your money. Rather, when you hear a great news announcement about a stock or other investment, and that news emotionally prompts you to open a position, *stop*. Take a look at a three-month chart and see if the investment hasn't already moved in the direction of the news. If it has, it is quite probable that the edge you were looking for has already disappeared. If it has, and you still want in, wait for three days after the news. By then, it's all in the price of the stock, and you can decide if you really want to own it or not.

In practice this means that *sometimes* ABC Widgets will move from $28 to $32 on the news and will continue to $38 shortly thereafter. That happens when you wait. It is Gallea's first law of news that if you wait, the stock goes higher, and if you buy, it goes lower. But, more often than not, you'll save yourself from those high and dry purchases that leave you with a loss and no catalyst to drive the investment in your direction.

BUYING IS
THE EASY PART.

You would think that opening and closing are the same thing. One is just the flip side of the other. Commissions are the same. Same position, same market. Yet it never seems to work out that way. It's been my experience that closing a position is three times more difficult than opening one. There are several reasons for this.

First, you can always count on someone ready to sell you what she has, but you can't always count on someone buying what *you* have. And the more you want to get out of something, the more difficult the market makes it for you to do so. This is especially true during a market panic, when cash is at a premium. If you want some of Mr. Market's cash, he's going to want to get as many shares or units or whatever that you hold for his cash. So he marks down the price and makes it hard on you.

Second, the decision to close is always more difficult than the decision to open. Whether buying to close a short position or selling to close a long one, the judgment to terminate is one that either admits to a mistake or concludes that further profit is problematic. Coming to either conclusion is more difficult than simply deciding to buy something that appears to have value. It's easy to purchase a stock for $25 that is down from an $80 high, but after the stock moves to $40, consider how difficult it is to decide whether $40 is a new top, and if so, that it should be sold. You fix on that $80 reference point when you buy and when you sell. Nevertheless it's harder on the sell side.

Third, good closing technique means you'll be moving alone, ahead of the crowd. If you wait for the crowd to tell you to close, the price will already have been either marked up (if you're short) or marked down (if you're long). Clearly, you want to close before everyone picks up on what you see, but that means solitary analysis and going against the grain. That's hard to do.

Despite this, most investors take the closing decision very lightly when opening and, in most cases, don't really give it any thought at all. The lesson to be learned from this is that you need to factor this difficulty into your strategy, and since closing is much more difficult than opening, you should think at least twice about buying anything that requires an agonizing mind-twister to get you into the trade. If the opening is tough, consider the Mount Everest you will confront at the close.

GREED—

Pigs Get Slaughtered

TREES DON'T GROW
TO THE SKY.

I'm not trying to transform this book into a gardening journal here. I'm simply trying to say that great stocks don't remain great forever. When was the last time you heard anything about Packard Motors? Indeed, General Electric is the only member of the original Dow Jones Industrial Average still on the list.

Stocks, as representative of the businesses underlying them, tend to be cyclical in nature. They have a great ride as the business takes off; then when the business cools, as it inevitably does, they cool as well. There is no straight line to heaven. It's more of a roller coaster than anything else.

The next time you fall in love with a stock and believe it's going to go straight up, just remember that when the roller coaster makes that big ascent, it rolls right over into that horrible, zero-gravity plunge.

EASY COME;
EASY GO.

Greed may be good, but even Gordon Gekko, the evil speculator in the movie *Wall Street*, understood that there were times when it made sense to take some profits and run. This is especially true when you reap a huge, unexpected gain in a very short time (let's say, 80 percent in a month).

When we buy a stock, most of us have a general idea of the return we're expecting. We have a rough price target and some expectation of when that target might be reached. For example, if a company's earnings are increasing at an average of 15 percent each year, and the stock's price tends to move in lockstep with earnings growth, the price of those shares should double in a bit less than five years.

If you buy that stock for $50 per share (let's say it's a drug company), you'd expect that it would double to $100 in five years. Now, assume that a few months later, the takeover of another drug company touches off a mini-mania in pharmaceutical stocks, and your shares rocket to $88. What should you do? What you should do is sell your shares.

Yes, I know your target was $100. That's irrelevant. The market has just handed you a delightful gift. Don't be rude. Take it.

DON'T CHASE
THE LAST DOLLAR.

What this means is that you'll never buy at the absolute bottom and you'll never sell at the absolute top. If you should ever be lucky enough to do so, and begin to think that it was skill and that you're very good, or that your neat little trading system just reached the sublime perfection of Nirvana, STOP! Don't make another move! You are a danger to yourself and everyone around you.

One of the most frustrating things that happens to investors is to follow a stock with the intention of purchase. Before the courage is summoned to do so, it moves. It happens to professionals all the time. In 2000, Waste Management (WMI) caught my eye. Bottom fisher that I am, I like a stock that had cratered from a high of $60 only to languish around $14. Many of its problems revolved around a faulty computer system (almost always a one-time, fixable problem), but a new CEO made it an interesting situation.

BAM! Before I could buy the stock, the company announced earnings ahead of consensus estimate, and the stock went up $3 to $17. Damn! OK, I said to myself, what I want the stock to do is to drop back to $14 so I can buy it.

Get used to it. You'll never catch the very top when you sell, and you won't grab the very bottom when you buy. The best you can do is to buy in a zone of reasonable value and then sell in a zone of unreasonable value—that is, when full value has been priced into the stock.

Waste Management? A cold shower brought me to my senses, and I bought the stock at $16⅜. Eventually, I sold it at $24, and it later drifted up into the high 20s.

NEVER TAKE A LOSS ON A STOCK IN WHICH YOU HAVE A PROFIT.

At the very least, set a stop-loss that preserves some profit on a winner. Profits in the market are difficult enough to come by. Once you have one, it is simply not acceptable to let that profit turn into a loss.

Investors do that simply because their greed gets the best of them. Unhappy with a modest profit, they hold on too long, often in the face of obviously deteriorating fundamentals, until it is simply too late.

Even if you take out a profit of 10 cents per share, do it. Get into the habit of never allowing a profit to turn into a loss. Not only is the loss harmful to your portfolio, but it can be devastating to your frame of mind.

BULLS MAKE MONEY,
BEARS MAKE MONEY,
PIGS GET SLAUGHTERED.

Yes, you say, but what about the cats and dogs? And salamanders? And newts? Our investing heritage doesn't have any metaphors for salamanders and newts, but the lexicon is rife with references to bulls and bears and pigs.

You see, an investor who is generally bullish on the market can make money. There has been a generally rising tide to stock prices for the past 125 years, and as long as the United States and the world at large continue to develop economically, this should continue. So, even if you're not Warren Buffett and all of your stock picks aren't gems, the rising tide will often bail you out of a bad situation.

Conversely, bears can make money too. A dyed-in-the-wool perma-bear is usually swimming upstream against a rising market, but the good ones (who are few and far between) can find stocks to short that will go down, so they make money too.

And within the confines of bulls and bears, there are all kinds of bulls and bears. Some make their money reading charts, others use astrology (I'm not kidding), and still others analyze balance sheets, income statements, and earnings reports to divine the future. The good ones, in whatever category, make money too.

But it's the pigs who get slaughtered. It's the investor who loads up on a single position and crosses his fingers and waits for that big move that will carry him home. It's the investor who has a full position in a commodity, and the contract moves in his favor, and he responds by loading up past all reasonable and prudent risk. These are the pigs, and they are slaughtered with distressing regularity.

Making money in the market, money that sticks, is a long, drawn-out, slogging affair. You get three yards and a cloud of dust on most every play. Once in a while you can throw a completion for 10 or 20 yards and, very rarely, a long pass. But you rarely get a Hail Mary. And if you ever do, it usually ruins you and makes you a pig, utterly hooked by the long shot that came home. Your greed loads up your arm and you fling the ball 60 yards downfield, where Mr. Market intercepts your pass and gleefully dances right past you into the end zone.

Don't be a pig. Be a bull. Be a bear if you must. But don't be a pig.

INTEREST
RATES—
Fractions Count

Don't Fight
the Fed.

Momentum investors are those who buy stocks going up because they believe they'll continue to go up. Put another way, they believe that a body in motion tends to stay in motion. While there may be some truth in that, just remember that a body in motion tends to eventually hit something. And, in the markets, that something is the granite-and-marble edifice known as the Federal Reserve.

The Fed was created in 1913 to regulate the United States money supply—that is, to run monetary policy. It's supposed to lean against inflation and recession. So when times are tough, it moves toward making money easy to get, and when good times bring on inflation, it leans against that by making money harder to get in an effort to cool demand for goods and services.

Now, the Fed has all the cards. When you play poker with the Fed, just remember that it's the dealer and the house, and gets to look at all the cards before it deals them. So, if you're smart, you won't fight the Fed. Everyone says that the chairman of the Federal Reserve is a very powerful person. Guess what? They're right. Did you ever get anywhere fighting very powerful people at their own game?

Don't be loopy. When the Fed is easing up on the interest rate throttle, the wind is at your back, and your odds of stock market success have risen. When the Fed is tightening, it's not really encouraging you to stick your neck out. Just remember that when it deals you a 7, a queen, a 4, a 10, and a 2, look across the table. What do you see? The chairman of the Federal Reserve, holding his cards close to his vest, with an enigmatic smile on his face.

INTEREST RATES DO MATTER.

The higher interest rates go, the less attractive stocks are. When the Federal Reserve Board doggedly raised interest rates during the past tech mania, lobotomized investors kept repeating a curious mantra, "Interest rates don't matter. Buy stocks."

Curious, because without exception, prolonged bouts of Federal Reserve interest rate increases have never boosted stock prices. As we saw in 2000, this can be difficult for some people to understand. In reality, the idea isn't difficult—at some point, interest rates on bonds become compelling, so you sell stocks to buy bonds.

To make this clear, here's a littles quiz:

1. What is the lowest interest rate on seven-year Treasury notes that would cause you to sell all of your stocks and buy the Treasury notes?

2. Now, what is the highest interest rate on the same seven-year Treasury notes that would cause you to sell all of your notes and buy stocks?

This interesting little exercise should point out a couple of things to you:

- At some point, interest rates will rise enough to cause you to sell all of your stocks.

Lesson: As interest rates rise, more and more people are willing to sell stocks and buy bonds.

- At some point, interest rates will fall enough to make stocks attractive to you again.

Lesson: As interest rates fall, more and more people are willing to sell bonds and buy stocks.

- The interest rate that causes you to sell all of your stocks is always higher than the interest rate that causes you to sell all of your bonds.

Lesson: As interest rates rise, it takes a higher rate to make you sell stocks than it does to make you sell bonds.

You might find that it takes 10 percent to make you sell all of your stocks, but it only takes, say, 7 percent to get you out of bonds. So, as interest rates rise, stocks become less attractive, which should be a warning signal that stocks may be in for a rough time.

UTILITIES AND INTEREST RATES—
TWO ENDS OF THE SEESAW

When interest rates go higher, utility stocks tend to fall. Utilities are hypersensitive to interest rates. Traditionally, they are the first of the three Dow averages to signal the market move ahead, be it up or down. Why is this so?

Historically, the utility averages were composed of electric utility stocks. Over the years, this has been modified a bit as utilities have increasingly moved beyond their traditional plug-in-power businesses. Today, many utilities are a conglomeration of other businesses (either acquired or built) to diversify away from a reliance on power generation.

However, it is fair to say that utilities are still sensitive to two over-riding market influences: interest rates and energy prices.

Utilities need to borrow money to fund capital improvements (build plants and upgrade equipment) and make more money when energy prices (the cost of oil and gas) are falling or low. In a low-interest-rate and low-energy-price environment, utilities can earn maximum profit margins. Those fat margins are reflected in rising dividend yields and rising utility prices.

When interest rates are rising, and energy prices are rising due to high demand in a fully stoked economy, utility investors sense a squeezing of profit margins and drive down utility stock prices, even as the broad market averages climb higher.

So, when you see the utility stock averages begin to fall—especially after a long bull market run—stop, drop, and roll. The market may be on fire, but utilities may be signaling the end of the party and the beginning of a hangover.

WATCH THOSE
CURVES.

When the yield curve inverts, a down market often follows. First, let us define an inverted yield curve. In an inverted yield curve, short-term interest rates are higher than long-term interest rates. For instance, the 2-year Treasury might be trading at 6.1 percent, while the 10-year fetches 5.9 percent. This inversion in the yield curve is generally caused by the Federal Reserve ratcheting up short-term interest rates to slow the economy.

The effect of raising short-term interest rates is to make borrowing more expensive. This more expensive borrowing creates several ripple effects through the economy. Corporations will find marginal expansion projects unprofitable with the higher cost of money and therefore shelve them. Individuals will postpone large purchases requiring credit. Automobiles and homes become more expensive due to higher costs, so purchases are curtailed.

Now all of this has the effect of slowing business, which ultimately reduces corporate profits. This reduction in corporate profits is anticipated by the stock market. So the Fed raises interest rates and some investors have a difficult time understanding why stocks go down while the economy continues to hum. It is much like the fighter who is hit with a big punch but experiences a delayed reaction. He might fight on for a few seconds and then go down.

An inverted yield curve, as a signal of Fed tightening, should not be ignored. Generally, you want to lighten up on your portfolio. Sometimes, if the Fed's hand is too heavy, the economy can slip into recession and a bear market can follow. Even if it's not a recession, the effect of the slowing economy still will be felt in stock prices.

When the yield curve moves toward inversion, cash is king. And, as the inversion reverts back to a more normal sloping curve, stocks (especially interest-sensitive stocks) will tend to rebound. The current yield curve is published every day in the credit column of *The Wall Street Journal*. I look at that chart daily. It's a reminder to me of where monetary policy is. When that curve inverts, I am especially cautious on new stock commitments.

MARKETS—
The Only Game in Town

You've Got to Love
Those Inefficient,
Efficient Markets.

There's a great debate among professionals about the so-called efficient market hypothesis. Many people—especially academics—believe that owning index funds is the only way to go. I, too, believe markets are efficient—long-term. I also fervently believe there are short-term inefficiencies, or aberrations, an investor can profitably exploit. Many studies support the notion that different techniques (buying low price/earnings or low price/sales stocks are two) can be used to beat the market. Exploiting these inefficiencies is where the money is made.

WATCH THE
SMART MONEY.

Since the market is always trying to confuse me and knock me off my game, one trick I've learned to stay on track is to watch the smart money.

Who is the smart money? You know some of them. Value investor Warren Buffett. Movers and shakers such as Kirk Kerkorian. Consummate professionals such as bond guru Bill Gross of PIMCO. You would be surprised how often they speak their mind about the markets, which lets you in on their thinking about what they see and what they are doing.

I think it's especially important to pay attention when one of these people offers a market opinion that I think strange or one with which I have fundamental disagreement. I believe these people are smarter than I am. They have these things figured out. It's what makes them great.

So, if I think interest rates are heading higher, and Bill Gross says they're not, I pay attention. What does he see that I don't? If the chairman of the Federal Reserve expresses a concern about inflation, and I don't see it, I should listen to him—he has the power. If Kirk Kerkorian takes a large position in a company, I might want to follow along, especially if it makes a little sense to me.

You see, such people have proven track records. Time and again, events have borne out their judgments. So, when I'm confused about the markets or feeling uneasy, I do a bit of research. What is Warren Buffett saying about stock prices? How does Bill Gross feel about interest rates? What is Kirk Kerkorian buying?

More often than not, these people illuminate passages that are dark to my eyes and, in that illumination, show me the way.

THE MARKET HAS
A MIND OF ITS OWN.

Investors often fall into the trap of believing that because they have carefully worked out a market forecast, the market will follow that forecast. Then, when the market deviates from that forecast, they "tweak" their view in an attempt to align it with what is actually happening.

As the market deviates more and more, they continue to adjust and, in frustration, pile position on top of position as if their actions will force the market to match their view of the world.

No matter how carefully we work, the market has its own mind. It goes where it will. We do not control it and we cannot usually divine the path that it will follow. No matter how hard we try, no matter how much effort we expend, as often as not events will take their own turn and ignore us completely.

Once we recognize this, it is much easier to work within the market, because by recognizing that the markets will go their own way and that our prognosticating will have no effect on them, we can remain flexible and quick to recognize when we are wrong.

There is nothing more frustrating than to feel that you really do have the truth figured out, only to have other investors ignore you and push the market in the opposite direction. On the other hand, if you know that this will happen and that such occurrences are frequent, then you won't set your opinions in concrete. You'll admit that as often as not you'll be wrong, and you'll stay light on your feet.

THE MARKETS ANTICIPATE
AND DISCOUNT.

If you don't think that the markets are smarter than you and I are, con-sider this: If you want to know how cold it will be in Florida this winter to decide whether or not to bring your sweater, don't go to the Weather Channel. Instead, look at the March or May orange juice contract trad-ing on the New York Board of Trade.

If the weather is going to be cold, you'll see the concern about crop damage in the price of the contract. Conversely, if a freeze is unlikely, OJ might be making new contract lows.

If the freeze hits, the news will be immediately put into the price of orange juice. At this point, the smart money, having correctly antici-pated the freeze, will be selling their contracts at a profit to those who just saw it on TV and want to make some money. Put another way, if you want to trade orange juice on a freeze that might happen in February, you had better start investing the previous October. The market begins to sniff it out up to four months in advance.

I'm telling you about orange juice because it is a story you'll remember. When you think orange juice, you'll think anticipation and discounting. It is a very healthy way to remember this law of the markets.

A MARKET TOP IS WHEN YOUR INVESTMENTS STOP GOING UP. A MARKET BOTTOM IS WHEN YOUR INVESTMENTS STOP GOING DOWN.

We often confuse ourselves by spending too much time worrying about "the market," or what other people are doing, or what is currently hot or cold. The only real thing to you as an investor is what your own positions are doing.

You can read endless analyses of whether or not the market has peaked. Ditto for market bottoms. The analyses will often be well thought out (although, as you know, they often will be contradictory).

The market, you see, doesn't know about your investment style. If your style is to short the grain market whenever you possibly can, then a rise or fall in the general commodity market is irrelevant to your position. What is relevant to your position is the movement of grain prices. Palladium, platinum, or crude oil prices are not a consideration, except only peripherally—they may be evidence of a general deflation in commodity prices.

Ah, but you say, "The odds are on my side when we have deflation and falling commodity prices." Ah, but I say, "Wrong!" The amount of rain falling in the Midwest has very little to do with the price of energy. The demand for grain being what it is (fairly constant), it's the weather that makes or breaks you in grains. The fact that crude oil is falling doesn't mean that grains are going to follow. A drought in Kansas ignores a glut of crude in Riyadh.

Make a point of focusing on what is real to your position. A top or bottom in a larger market helps give you some overall context for your activity, but little else.

MAKE 'EM
PROVE IT.

The speed of market information is so rapid that we usually don't slow down enough to say, "Prove it!" And so we act on bad information or opinion.

Here's an example: During the 1998–99 parabolic ascent of technology stocks, many market pundits struggled to make sense of why so many stocks had gone through the roof. That is, rather than doubt the judgment of investors pushing stocks to nosebleed levels, they concluded that since traditional measures such as P/E ratios couldn't explain the move, those traditional measures were no longer useful.

I hate to kill the buzz, but I think that when people suddenly brush away decades of considered research, academic effort, Nobel prizes, and basic economic theories, someone should say, "Prove it!"

A DEPRESSED MARKET ALWAYS COMES BACK—EVENTUALLY.

Even in the dead of night, the dawn is rushing toward you.

Sometimes we forget that the investments we make are inevitably tied to the societies and peoples who create them. Thus, we often lose sight of the fact that almost without exception, there is a turn in the tide that brings a depressed market back, just as the turn in the tide will depress a roaring bull market.

No matter how pessimistic investors may have been about the Japanese stock market in the 1990s, it was still an irrefutable fact that the Japanese people and their island weren't going to disappear beneath the waves of the Pacific. No matter what the level of stock prices, there were still millions upon millions of industrious and well-educated people getting up every morning and making a nation run. It's such a simple thing that we forget it.

Yet, as we read bearish commentary upon bearish commentary, the mindset of the investing public (professional and amateur alike) became rigid in its view: The Japanese were never coming back. As a result, when the tide actually turned in 1999 for a tradable rally, nearly everyone wouldn't or couldn't believe it. It could have been an easy thing to take the point of view that after 10 years of horrible investment returns, maybe, just maybe, the Japanese were due for a change.

The next time you run across a really depressed market—one that has been that way for years—you can remind yourself that it's darkest before the dawn, or the dawn is rushing to you, or anything else that reminds you of the cyclical nature of markets.

LOOK
AROUND YOU.

Here's the rule for investors: Absolutely, positively, don't be xenophobic. A good friend of mine is a British representative to a major European money management house (to us, they're a "firm," to the Brits, a "house"). At any rate, my friend finds Americans' attitudes toward sports infuriating. "Look, outside of the Americas, no one except the Japanese cares about bloody baseball. And football, to the world, is soccer and billions of people follow that." Blah, blah, blah . . .

My friend, of course, is right, but that's another story for another time.

The point is that this can carry over to Americans' views of investing. With so many good companies and opportunities here, why pay any attention to the overseas markets? Setting aside the argument for diversification (and that's a strong one), there is an aspect to foreign markets that always has my attention.

The relationship between the U.S. dollar and foreign currencies is something to watch. We've had many years of dollar strength and have come to believe that the world views the dollar as a fiat world currency. But we should remember that a strong currency encourages foreigners to buy dollars and invest in our markets. So the strength of the dollar provides additional buying power for our markets.

At some point, the dollar will reverse (eventually, all currencies do). The reversal may be a minor blip, or it may be a major trend reversal—no one knows. I do know that if you don't pay attention to it, you'll find out only when it's a front-page item and losses have been taken.

You may not believe that this is an important issue, but consider this: In October 1987, an already nervous market was unsettled over a weekend when a dispute between the U.S. Secretary of the Treasury and the Germans about interest rate policy broke into the open. A crash followed and many observers laid at least some of the blame on that open dispute.

I always watch the overseas markets—not only because I have money invested there, but also because monetary policy in Japan or Europe and the effects it can have on our markets are important. If the European Central Bank raises its lending rate, my eyebrow may go up. If the Japanese allow a bank failure, I "hmmm . . ." over my coffee. I make all sorts of funny faces and noises in the morning as I look at the overnight movement of foreign markets.

THE MARKET MOVES
TOWARD MAXIMUM ACTIVITY.

If you're not sure where the market is going to go, just ask yourself what move would create the greatest amount of activity. More often than not, the answer will correctly point the way for you.

You see, one way the market beats us down is by whipping us back and forth, in and out of our positions. It seeks to rattle the greatest number of people as often as possible. To do this, it moves in ways to create maximum activity.

Consider a stock that has been in a three-month correction, has now moved up, and is just below its 52-week high. You just know that if it can hit that high and move above it, that will create the greatest amount of activity. Those in the stock will sell, fearing the stock will hit resistance at that high, and those who have been watching it will buy on the breakout as the high is taken out. From there, the greatest activity is created by the stock falling back below the high. Many of those who just bought the stock will bail out in fear, creating more activity, and those who missed the breakout will buy the dip.

Can you see how that works? You would be amazed how often this rule can accurately forecast the next near-term move. Whenever I'm not sure about the direction of an investment, I just ask myself what move would create the greatest volume, action, and activity. The answer often points the way.

EVEN EXPERTS
CAN BE WRONG.

Many investors underestimate earnings when markets are rising, and they overestimate them when markets are falling. It is a constant amazement to me that a company can consistently beat investors' estimates by a few pennies per share each quarter. After years of doing this, you would think that investors would estimate earnings at a few pennies a share above their real estimates and, therefore, be more accurate. It never seems to happen.

Part of the reason is that people tend to underestimate the effects of both good things going well and bad things getting worse. Whether you're a company or an individual, when you're on a roll, there are two things you can bank on: first, that you'll be surprised by things getting even better; and, second, that things will reverse, often when you least expect them to.

I wish there were a general rule that you could apply to these things. For instance, wouldn't it be nice if it could be proved that two positive earnings surprises are always followed by a third? Alas, such is not the case. These earnings surprises or disappointments are, well, surprises. And by their very nature, you can't anticipate a surprise!

The best advice I can give you is

1. Since you can't forecast an earnings surprise, don't spend a lot of time doing so.

2. Just because a company has been surprising doesn't mean that will continue to be so.

IT'S EARNINGS THAT DRIVE THE MARKET.

As I observe the markets from day to day, I get bogged down in all sorts of detail. I'm drowned in information as a fire hose of opinion cascades down on me. I do everything I can to limit the avalanche, but it is simply too persistent.

What this leads to is confusion. If I'm not careful, I start losing the forest for the trees. I find myself focusing on smaller and smaller details, somehow feeling that if I could just yank one more nugget out of the stream, all would be clear. Of course, the more I do that, the more confused I can become.

A trick I've learned is to simply remind myself that over time, it is earnings that drive the price of a stock and drive the stock market (a collection of stocks). You'd be amazed at how often that can snap you back from a line of thinking that's taking you down the wrong road.

A new CEO is named to a company in trouble. Often, investors cheer the change and bid up the stock in a frenzy of optimism. Now, a company in trouble with a new CEO is the kind I like to buy. It's a contrarian play based on the new catalyst to change the course of the company. That is to say, I don't need a whole lot of encouragement to buy.

But as I watch that scenario unfold, I keep repeating to myself, it's earnings that drive the price. That reminds me that no matter how qualified the new CEO, if the potential for a turnaround isn't there, it's not a stock to buy.

You can't roll
back the sea.

Like King Canute, you can't roll back the sea. King Canute the Great was a Viking king in the 11th century. His courtiers flattered him so much that they claimed he could command the tides of the sea to go back. As a religious man, Canute had a realistic view of what kings could accomplish. To prove his point, he had his throne placed at the shore and sat on it, even as he commanded the incoming tides to recede. Of course they didn't and he had made his point: Know your limitations.

It's a story worth remembering. Ultimately, we are all powerless to stop the tide of the market. It goes where it will—no matter how much we may will it otherwise, we will have no effect. You may want and need to have the market accommodate you, but it will go its own way.

And it has been my experience that the more you need a market to move in a certain way, the less likely it will be to do so.

IT'S A TOUGH WAY
TO MAKE A LIVING.

One of the crueler jokes is that people have come to believe that making money in the market is easy. This silliness is born and bred in a bull market, when it really is easy to make money. Now, this should not be confused with keeping the money, which is a completely different thing.

Just consider the circumstances of the market and what you face trying to make money in it:

- Your competitors are numerous, have more money than you, and in the aggregate, are smarter and have greater staying power.

- Thousands of them devote every waking hour to finding opportunities. Thousands more went to the best schools and have advanced degrees directly bearing on the subject. Whatever they may lack in instinct or courage is made up for by thousands of others who have excellent instincts and courage and deep pockets to boot.

- The government will take anywhere from 20 to 40 percent of your profits when you are right.

- Your emotions will work overtime against you, as will the other circumstances of your life that make concentration and consistent effort difficult.

- You have almost no ability to guess the direction of the market or which sectors or specific investments will be this year's winners.

Now all of this doesn't mean that you shouldn't try. Nor does it mean that you should abandon hope of earning money in the markets. What it does mean is that any thought of actually earning a living from the markets is a long shot at best. It's one thing to sit through periods of losses when the money at risk is money you'll need in 20 years when you retire. It's quite another to have the grocery money at risk. The difference in pressure is enormous, and it is that pressure to perform, whether or not the market will accommodate you, that is the root of so much investment failure.

If you are thinking about quitting your day job to make money in the market, think very hard. As a matter of fact, don't think about it at all.

OPTIONS—

Hedging Your Bet

MAKE TIME YOUR ALLY—
SELL OPTIONS.

One of the basic attributes of a listed options contract is that it has an expiration date. This obvious fact has a very important bearing on how you should handle options. To make money over the long haul, you want to be a seller, not a buyer, of options.

An option is a wasting asset. Every day, as it approaches expiration, its value will decline, all other things being equal. It is not generally a good investment strategy to invest capital in a wasting asset.

As an option seller, you transfer that value erosion to the buyer of the option. With IBM trading at 100, you sell a January 100 call with two months remaining for $8.00. On average, over that 60 days, the option will decline in price due to time erosion by about 13 cents every day or $8.00 per contract. So, if the stock remains unchanged (and they often tend to do that), you win and the buyer loses.

Let's think about that. If the stock does nothing, you win. If the stock declines, you also win (at least on the option). You can even win if the stock rises by less than $8.00. So, in almost every likely scenario, you win. As a matter of fact, you win on the option three out of four times:

- If the stock goes down, you win.

- If the stock remains the same, you win.

- If the stock goes up a little bit, you win.

- If the stock goes up a lot, you lose.

The odds are 75 percent in your favor. That's a good scenario.

On a put sale, you've got the same thing in reverse. If you sell a put, you win if the stock goes up, remains the same, or goes down a little bit. Same odds—75 percent in your favor.

I am an active seller of options for my clients' accounts as well as my own, both as a naked seller (for myself when I don't own the underlying asset) and as a covered call writer (for clients). In my experience, options trades are profitable about 70 percent of the time—a real-world result very close to the theoretical number of contracts expiring worthless.

Small investors tend to be options buyers because

1. To be a seller, you need collateral to hold down the position.

2. Options can be a risky game. A stock can move heavily against you, creating substantial position loss.

3. Most investors underestimate the burden that time erosion imposes on the option buyer.

As a result, for many investors, selling options isn't a good strategy. However, if nothing else, an understanding of how time erodes an option position may, I hope, temper your enthusiasm for the outright speculative purchase of options.

THINK,
"EXPIRES WORTHLESS."

If you're a seller of options, your perfect world comes together on expiration day when every single option you're short expires worthless. It's the holy grail of option writing and what you want as your goal.

Of course, you say, if the option expires worthless, then you receive maximum profit. That's why you want to do it. That's true. Yet there is a more subtle but equally important idea at work here.

When you think in terms of expiring worthless as you put on positions, you tend toward higher-probability strategies. If you want every short position to expire worthless, then you find yourself seeking call and put writes that are out of the money. You don't try to be too directional in your strategy. Rather, you're looking for high-volatility options positions where it's a stretch to believe that the stock or index can go in the money by date of expiration.

Generally, you find yourself writing several strikes away from the current price, where the meat of favorable probability is for you. Over time, it is a viable strategy.

One caveat: The further away from the current market the option strike is, the less likely it is to have value at expiration. Taken to its extreme, you'd wind up writing options far out of the money and taking in dimes for the effort. This is not a good strategy.

A BUYER OF OPTIONS NEEDS
TO CLEAR HIGH HURDLES.

Most individual investors are purchasers of options. As a purchaser of options, you have several hurdles to clear that, in combination, make it very difficult to earn a consistent profit.

First, the underlying investment (a stock, commodity, or currency, for instance) has to move substantially in your direction. If you are long a call, it must go up enough to cover the cost of the call and still leave room for profit. A long put position means that the underlying investment has to do the opposite—fall, and fall far enough to get you a profit.

Second, it must move within the time frame of your option. If you've purchased three-month calls, you need to see that movement within the three months until expiration. Gallea's first law of options states that the underlying investment will begin a big move the day after your option expires.

Third, time is against you as a holder of an option. Every second, every minute, every hour, and every day works against you as the option moves closer and closer to expiration.

Finally, options profits are taxed as short-term capital gains, so you have a partner. Uncle Sam is more than happy to ride along with you and put his hand out for nearly half every time you score.

Combine all of this with commissions and spreads on trades and you can see why I'm generally not in favor of buying options. Strategies that call for purchases of options are generally low-probability strategies. The odds are stacked against you. If you play long enough, the market tends to win.

There is, perhaps, only one exception to this: if you purchase U.S. Treasury bills and use the interest to purchase options. This can be a profitable long-term strategy, because every year, you replace your losses with more T-bill interest. However, since this strategy has about as much excitement as watching grass grow, my guess is that you'll take a pass.

And so, while you may, from time to time, speculate using the purchase of a call or put option, I would counsel against consistently using a buy-side strategy in the options market.

DON'T RUSH.

Too many options players rush into the markets with a market order. Getting a market price is often very expensive, especially in options that are illiquid.

For instance, I recently saw an index option quoted at 11½ bid, 14½ offered. Now that was an option I wanted to sell, since naked option writing is my preferred trading vehicle. At a bid of 11½, the option was significantly underpriced—I wasn't getting a large enough premium for the risk of being naked the option. Of course, the 14½ offer was overpriced—a buyer would be paying too much.

I couldn't blame the market maker. He needs that spread to protect himself, since it is a position he may have to stay in until expiration. He can't expect a buyer or seller at his price on an illiquid option. What to do?

I simply split the bid/offer and put in a limit order at $13, minus ¼ or ½ as a nod to the market maker. And so, my order went in at $12¾. The order sat there all day, and then, just before the close, for whatever reason, someone bit and I sold the option at my price. Since I was selling three contracts, that meant an additional $375 in my account. Do that 20 times and it's a cool $7,500 difference.

Was I worried that the market would move away from me? Sure. Always. But I didn't have to sell the option position. I wasn't long the options. It was a new position for me. My attitude was simple: Give me my price, or I'll just go look for something else. There is always another trade to do.

At 12¾, the option was priced closer to fair value, so the market finally cleared at that price. But it is a good lesson to learn. When the bid/offer is wide, split the difference, give them a little bit to work with, and let the order sit at your price. You'd be surprised how often you get an execution.

IF YOU SELL OPTIONS,
SELL OVERVALUED OPTIONS.

In all investing, you're always trying to sell an overvalued asset and buy an undervalued asset. It is so with option selling, whether you are selling covered or naked options.

There are two ways in which an option can be overvalued. Every book ever written about options will tell you to sell options in which the implied volatility expressed by the option price is historically high. This sound advice works especially well when you're swinging around 100 contracts at a clip. A 50-cent difference in fair value on the option translates into an easy $5,000. But, if you're only selling three contracts, that 50 cents is only $75.

Now, with $75 here and $75 there, pretty soon you're talking serious money. But the point is that the overvaluation you may see is not as important as overvaluation from this: *The most overvalued option is the one on the wrong side of the stock.*

If the stock is trading at $35, a 60-day $35 strike call option trading at $2.00 is completely overvalued if the stock is about to go down to $30 over the next two months. That call will expire worthless.

Conversely, the volatility valuation may show that call to actually be only worth $1.50, but if the stock is about to rise to $40, then the call is actually very cheap.

The point is that the direction of the underlying instrument is the greatest determinant of the valuation of option premiums. It is correct trading practice to check the implied volatility of the option to seek those options trading rich to their historic volatility. In the process, just don't forget that if you get the direction of the underlying instrument wrong, volatility analysis will be of little help.

Valuation in options comes in two forms. Keep straight in your mind the more important of the two.

BALANCE THE RISK.

As a naked seller of options, you don't own the underlying stock on call options you sell, and you must be willing to buy the stock of put options in which you are short—which means, have the stock literally "put" to you.

Now naked option selling is an inherently risky business. You are taking on the potential for a large loss in exchange for a finite and limited gain. Strictly from a correct trading posture, this is not a strategy to pursue. Nonetheless, it can be executed profitably.

The key to doing so is to balance your positions with out-of-the-money put and call sales that roughly reflect your view of the market. A couple of examples will help:

If you are neutral on the market, then you want to sell out-of-the-money puts and calls in roughly equal portions, as reflected by the delta of the positions. If you are short 1,000 delta points in calls, you want to be long 1,000 delta points in puts (which you do by shorting the puts since they have negative delta—short negative delta being the equivalent of long delta). Your delta position doesn't have to be exact, but it should be close and it should be actively monitored since deltas change as the underlying instrument changes.

Now, by selling both calls and puts, you can be fairly certain that about 50 percent of your short positions will expire worthless. If you sell out-of-the-money calls and puts on the same stock, then at least half will expire worthless. So you've already improved your profit odds.

Of course, if you sell calls on one stock and puts on another, it is entirely possible that you could have a loss on both sides of the equation.

Now, not only should you sell calls and puts on the same stocks, but you should diversify the underlying stocks by industry. You want to avoid a big move in a single industry ruining your balance sheet, which, in practice, might mean you sell combinations on a semiconductor stock, a bank stock, and an industrial stock, for instance. Or, simply sell a combination on an index such as the S&P 100 or NASDAQ Composite.

If you believe the market is going higher, then you might want to sell two puts for every call—you're leaning your positions in a way that reflects your view of the market. Conversely, you'll sell more calls than puts if you believe the market is going to be weak.

However, what you want to avoid is the big bet—selling only calls or selling only puts because you have a strong view of the market. You only have to be wrong once. You can get caught in a big updraft or downdraft that can leave you scrambling to unwind positions or redo them.

Remember that as a naked seller of options, your primary strength is the time erosion of option premium, not your view of the market. Indeed, it may be more beneficial to always assume the market will be unchanged and then create your options portfolios from that perspective, than to try to guess market movement and position options accordingly.

A $50 BOTTLE OF SCOTCH
OFFERS A LOT MORE QUALITY
THAN A $10 BOTTLE.

Generally speaking, I don't believe that you can make money with options selling for less than a dollar.

If you are a buyer of those options, you've probably bought an option far out of the money or with a very short time to expiration. Put another way, you need either a big move or a quick move in the security. Since securities stand still, on average, 70 to 80 percent of the time, the odds are four in five against you that the security will move enough to accommodate you. Any option buyer learns that the security never moves before your option expires, let alone within a few days.

"Well then," you say, "If the buyer of those options is almost a guaranteed loser, then I will be a seller and reap the rewards." If you do that, you'll find that in almost every case, you'll pocket the premium and emerge a winner. The problem, however, is that you're taking on a huge risk with a very small, finite gain. You're attempting to capture a $50 profit, but if you're wrong, you could experience a very large loss.

One of two things tends to happen. First, you get caught in a stock meltdown (if short puts) or an unanticipated big move to the upside (a takeover, for instance). Instantly, you've vaporized the profits on 20 or 30 successful options profits on one trade. And since you've got to sell a lot of fractional options in order to make some reasonable money, you're increasing your odds of getting caught short every time you write a position.

Finally, here's an intuitive truth: In life, cheap goods are generally not as good as expensive ones. A $50 bottle of Scotch offers a lot more quality than a $10 bottle. So it is with options. Cheap options can often be like cheap whiskey—you think you're enjoying yourself, but the hangover is just awful.

IN THE END,
IT'S THE DIRECTION THAT COUNTS.

For me, two wonderful things about the options market are its complexity and the strategies you can employ in it. The complexity is a compelling challenge that I never tire of.

In addition to making basic investment decisions about stocks and markets, you have to deal with several additional layers of complexity: (1) time erosion of the options, (2) multiple options strategies from which to choose, and (3) the elegant dance that is the combined effect of each of these options and stocks trading in concert with each other. It's all I can handle and more—and that's part of the fun.

But I also recognize that the first order of business is to make a profit, so a lot of my effort isn't particularly enjoyable, but it does help me earn a profit. Analyzing the relative value of one option against the other isn't what I'd call a high point, but it must be done. Multiplying the delta of an option against the number of contracts long or short and then combining all of that data must be done.

And of all the work that I have to do in an options environment, nothing is more important than getting the movement of the underlying instrument correct.

A simple example suffices. Let's say that I want to sell some naked puts on XYZ Widget, because its new B2B Widget will be, I believe, a huge winner and the stock is therefore underpriced. I analyze all of the XYZ Widget put options and finally find one that is unbelievably overpriced.

And so I sell 10 XYZ October 35 puts for $3, when the stock is trading at $36 with only three weeks to go until expiration.

The next morning, XYZ announces that the B2B Widget has a faulty demodulator in the fibrous analagram, so the stock plunges to $8. I have taken a huge hosing on the XYZ October 35 put options.

You see, I did sell the right option. The October 35s were over-priced *compared to other puts*, but I made a simple mistake: I got the movement of the underlying sstock completely wrong. Had I gotten that right, I could have been a *buyer* of those grossly overvalued October 35s and still made a bundle.

It is the movement of the underlying security upon which the option is based that is the key to successful options trading.

Get that right and you prosper.

AFTER EXTREME
HIGHS AND LOWS, TRADE OPTIONS.

Sometimes an event can change the investment landscape in a particular stock, sector, or index. In reaction, the underlying instrument jumps from lows or drops from highs. This is often a tradable event for the options seller.

Here are the keys to the technique:

1. Identify the extreme high or low and the clear change in outlook. Perhaps it was a surprise earnings warning, or it might have been a general collapse (or rally) caused by a fundamental event, such as war in the oil-rich Middle East.

2. Identify a short-term option to sell. For instance, you might iden-tify a top in the Widget index due to a major OSHA ruling ques-tioning the safety of the new Cha Cha Widget that has the industry buzzing. The index drops from a high of 800 to 775. Now clearly, the playing field has changed. The news tells you that (the ruling isn't an issue that will be cleared up quickly) and the price drop in the index tells you that.

Given the new, more cautious atmosphere, it is very unlikely that investors will push the Widget index to highs above 800, because that 800 high was set in an atmosphere of high optimism. In effect, 800 becomes the high bar.

The 30-day or 60-day 800 call option will generally retain too much premium relative to the chances of that option being profitable for the buyer. Therefore, you are a high-probability seller of that option. You sell the 30-day 800 call option on the index. This is a trade that often works, but you need to be sure that the atmosphere has indeed changed.

You will find a collapse in the option premium within a couple of weeks of the change, and you can close it out or let it go to expiration.

OPTIONS ARE NOT
FOR THE MATHEMATICALLY
CHALLENGED.

Many investors find options exciting and fascinating. The prospect of leverage and limited risk (for the buyer) offers many attractive opportunities for many strategies. The fact that so many investors lose money in the options markets reflects, to a great extent, a lack of understanding of how options actually work in the market.

In order to work successfully in the options markets, you need to have a thorough grounding in mathematics, including bell curve pricing assumptions, implied volatilities, and skew (when different options on the same stock trade at different price levels). Good options trading is all about calculating the odds, the mathematical probabilities of price movement, and the ever-changing aspects of option risk.

For those who find these concepts difficult to learn, or for those who find mathematics difficult, boring, or strange, the best advice is to leave options strategies alone. It's as though you were trying to negotiate a mortgage without understanding compound interest.

It is no coincidence that serious options traders have a battery of very sophisticated computer programs and models to assist them in their work. Whenever the other guy is pricing with a computer, it should give you pause. He isn't necessarily going to be right, but I'm not sure you should bet against him either.

PUT/CALL RATIOS—
A SOMETIME INDICATOR

There has been a lot written about put/call ratios over the years. As a contrarian, I believe that put/call ratios can convey important market information, but I admit, the record isn't clear on this point.

The put/call ratio is a simple computation used to gauge market sentiment. It divides the number of put contracts outstanding by the number of call contracts outstanding to arrive at a ratio. Let's say that there are

13,000 put contracts outstanding.

12,000 call contracts outstanding.

In this example, the put/call ratio is 1.08—108 put contracts outstanding for every 100 call contracts. Sometimes the calculation is done the other way, dividing the calls by the puts. We'd arrive at a call/put ratio of 0.92 (92 put contracts outstanding for every 100 call contracts).

The theory behind put/call ratios is quite simple. As a contrarian indicator, it would stand to reason that as investors became more and more bullish, they would not feel the need to purchase puts for protection on the positions they held. At the same time, we would expect to see an increase in the number of call contracts outstanding as investors began to speculate in call options, anticipating a market rise. We would expect the put/call ratio to decline:

11,500 put contracts outstanding.

14,000 call contracts outstanding.

This results in a put/call ratio of 0.82. The most popular put/call ratio is that for the S&P 100 (known as the OEX for its symbol) contracts on the Chicago Board Options Exchange (CBOE). As one of the most liquid options series on a broad market index, the put/call ratio on the OEX is a natural for computation since it can't be skewed or thrown off by a single large trade. The ratio is quoted in many financial publications, including *Barron's*.

So far, so good. Theory makes sense. However, before you rush out to buy your *Barron's* to begin tracking the put/call ratio, consider the real-world behavior of the put/call ratio. Here are four weekly consecutive ratios on the OEX as of this date:

1.11   1.54   0.81   1.14

During those four weeks, the S&P 500 was essentially unchanged.

It's quite beyond me how the put/call ratio, on its own, can be used as a reliable market-timing device. Like all contrasignal indicators, it can go deep into overbought or oversold territory during a particularly ferocious move and throw you off. Your put/call ratio may be screaming "sell" as the number of put contracts declines while the market relentlessly marches higher.

My best advice on the put/call ratio is this: Pay attention to it. Glance at it every week. Take a quick look at the recent trend. Make a mental note of it as a secondary indicator as you try to frame your view of the market. It's a piece of the puzzle, but not the corner piece.

NO STOCK GOES
IN A STRAIGHT LINE.

Nearly every book, brochure, and pamphlet about options says the same thing: Selling naked call options carries unlimited risk. I have not found that to be true.

At first blush, this strategy would seem to be fraught with the possibility of unlimited risk. After all, what if you had sold naked calls on a stock such as Microsoft or Cisco early in its history? Wouldn't those losses have devastated you? Wouldn't the relentless increase in those stocks have created huge losses?

Taken at face value, the answer would be yes. But closer examination reveals that the loss might not be as unlimited as you may think.

First, no stock goes in a straight line. No stock moves ever higher without correcting. And it is in those corrections that you have the opportunity to repair your position, to roll to different strike prices, to buy other stocks in the same industry to help mitigate the wrong-sided position you may be in.

In 1999, I decided to sell naked call options on four Internet stocks for my own portfolio (this is not a strategy I would ever recommend to a client). It takes a strong stomach, or a lack of brains, to sell calls on stocks in the midst of a rampant bull move, but that's exactly what I did. I decided that valuations on these stocks were unrealistic and that eventually they had to come back to earth.

My timing couldn't have been worse. As the mania for Internet stocks pushed these stocks to higher and higher levels, losses began to mount, at one point exceeding $100,000. Now, relative to the size of my account, these losses were bearable since I had followed Gallea's number one rule: Always keep each position small relative to your trading capital.

Therefore, as the calls went against me, deeper and deeper into the money, I simply rolled them forward. An October 100 call was rolled to a January 110 call for even money and I waited things out.

One by one, these stocks began to falter as the Internet mania wore itself out. Of course, I was worn out as well, having wrestled with these positions for nearly a year, and having nothing but losses and anxieties to show for the effort.

But then, as they dropped, losses began turning into breakeven, so I was able to exit them all, one by one with a profit. I would be the first to admit that they were dumb trades. I stood in front of a roaring train and got hit, not once, but month after month. My timing was terrible and I should have simply exited the positions at a 10 percent stop-loss or some such money management stop.

Sometimes you can be stubborn. Sometimes I can be very stubborn. In this case, the overvaluations were so extreme (I had penciled out the earnings and P/E multiples on the stocks going forward 10 years given the current growth rates) that I just knew I was going to be right. Eventually, sanity would prevail.

It did.

The moral of the story is this: Anyone, even a 20-year professional, can be incredibly stupid and dense. But I stood in front of perhaps the most parabolic rise in the history of the 20th-century markets, the wrong way, and came out with a profit.

Naked call selling has its risks. But the risk is not unlimited. By taking small positions, and only doing so on extremely overvalued stocks, you can survive and profit.

Finally, I should mention that all the while that was happening to me, I was long a lot of other stocks and so, on an overall basis, was making money.

Don't put all your eggs
in one basket.

Contrary to what you read, a naked seller of put options does not have "unlimited risk." When we think that through, we find a different sort of risk.

If you are a seller of puts, your risk is not unlimited. It is actually limited to the price of the underlying stock position. Let's say you are a naked seller of five XYZ Widget March 30 puts, with XYZ trading at $30. You receive $3.00 per option ($1,500 total). Now in this case, your risk is limited to $13,500. If XYZ goes to zero, the put option will be trading at $30 per option ($15,000). Subtract from that the option premium you received as a seller ($1,500) and you arrive at a potential loss of $13,500. That's not pretty, but it's not unlimited either.

Call options have a different risk profile. While the potential loss on a put option sale is limited by the price of the stock to zero, to the upside a stock can certainly increase by more than 100 percent. A $40 stock can't go below zero (for a $40 loss), but it can certainly go up a lot more than $40, so losses on naked call selling are a much different thing to handle, but it would be hard to argue that the risk is unlimited.

First, if you sell both calls and puts in balance, you'll often have profits on one side or the other. If the market rises and you generally have losses on your calls, you'll also have put profits to help reduce those losses.

Second, investors tend not to sell the same call, time after time, no matter what the loss. So you don't tend to hold the short call position long enough to experience multi–hundred-percent loss. As a matter of fact, if you simply insert a trading rule that does not allow you to sell a call again on the same stock for six months, you will avoid those very large losses—the stock needs time to gain warp speed.

Finally, if you use proper trading techniques and take small positions, even a short call that moves heavily against you will not decimate a properly diversified portfolio. For instance, if you have a $100,000 portfolio and limit your call selling to one contract per stock, a quick move in the underlying stock from $30 to $90 (a rare circumstance, to say the least) means a loss of $6,000 and would probably be mitigated by profits on other positions.

The risk in selling naked options is real. As a seller, you will experience large losses from time to time. It is inescapable. However, you need to put it all in perspective. The losses aren't unlimited and can be controlled to a great extent.

This illustrates yet again the need to take small positions to diversify risk and avoid big losses on a single position.

KEEP YOUR NET DELTA
POSITION FLAT.

In my option writing account, I keep detailed records, every day, of my net delta position. When writing (selling) naked options, you're betting on two ideas that, in combination, give you a good chance of success:

1. That great enemy of the option buyer, the premium decay resulting from the passage of time, becomes your ally.

2. The option buyer has to pick not only the direction of the move but also the extent of the move.

In order to further reduce the option buyer's chances of beating you, you want to sell both calls and puts, in roughly equal portions. If you do so *and* you are diversified, you have reasonably good odds that, on average, one side of the equation will expire worthless. If you are short calls and puts and the market rallies, your puts will generally lose value. In a market decline, the calls lose value, so the odds are increased in your favor.

And just to be sure that you use the pistol as well as the garrote, you want to sell out-of-the-money calls and puts, because you can profit on both sides if the market goes nowhere, which it does 70 to 80 percent of the time.

The key here is to not only measure your positions by the dollar amount you've sold, the value of the underlying stock or index, or even the number of contracts that you've sold short. The key is to also measure the delta of each position, add them up, and strive to keep the delta numbers on your short puts equal to the delta totals on your short calls.

Now, if the market moves higher, the deltas on your calls will increase, so you need to either buy back the calls or sell more puts. I tend to sell more puts (this is also the equivalent of trading with the trend) and vice versa.

This isn't an exact science, however. If I believe the market is going to decline, I'll have more calls sold than puts. If I believe a market rally is in the works, I'll overweight selling of puts. If the market moves in the way I anticipate, the deltas will generally shift into neutral, but I will have sold more premium away from market movement and so will improve my profits.

You can keep track of this with a simple spreadsheet. Going through this exercise on a regular basis will keep your options positions balanced. Doing so allows you to play on your two original ideas: the premium decay over time and the fact that the market must not only move but move heavily to put your positions into a loss. Remember that roughly half of them will still be profitable, thereby mitigating the losses.

The mistake many options writers make is to load up on one side or the other, selling only calls or only puts. By doing so, they're really just trying to call the direction of the market, rather than play a good option writing strategy.

SOMETIMES YOU HAVE TO
IGNORE THE EXPERTS.

Another thing that just about every options guide or book you'll ever read will expound upon is the idea of volatility skew, and every book will encourage you to find options whose pricing is out of line with volatility. Then you are encouraged to buy or sell those options whose implied volatility is out of line with others on the same stock. Presumably, you capture the premium when volatility returns to normal.

In theory, this is perfectly sound. In practice, your time is better spent trying to pick the right security or index to sell against. Here's why:

First, the advent of widely available high-speed search engines, searching in real time, means that options players have become highly efficient in finding any discrepancies and forcing them back into line by selling or buying into them.

Second, I think you'll find that to be profitable, you need to trade a lot of contracts (10 or more) to capture those small discrepancies.

Third, the bid/ask spread on those options is often very wide, and the volatility equation is based on prices that you probably can't get.

Fourth, options commentary usually comes from analysts working in the institutional marketplace, where commissions are lower and size is larger, say 50 contracts or more.

Finally, most options are fairly priced to volatility, so opportunities are relatively scarce.

Keep in mind that you've only got so much time to research and execute your options ideas, so you've got to put it to maximum and efficient use. Much more important than trying to find a mispriced option is to get the general direction of the security or index right. If the security moves in the direction you anticipate, the move in the option due to the movement in the underlying security will be much more pronounced than any movement in volatility pricing.

I've met traders who are successful options sellers. They tend to concentrate on finding the right security.

One more thing: If an option looks mispriced, there is probably a reason for it. You might not be able to see it now, but you will no doubt find out the reason once you enter the position. In my experience, the cost of gaining that knowledge is usually painful.

LOOK FOR
BIG REWARDS.

In order to maximize the return on your option writing, you want to compare the premium you're taking in with the amount of collateral your broker demands as good faith money to hold the position.

For instance, you may be looking at two index call writes with 30 days until expiration. One has a premium of $1,000 and a collateral requirement of $30,000, and the other a $1,500 premium and a collateral requirement of $40,000. Which do you take?

The $1,000 premium represents roughly a 3.3 percent return on the collateral for the 30 days or 40 percent annualized. The $1,500 premium works out to 3.75 percent or 45 percent annualized. All things being equal, you take the $1,500 premium trade.

Since there are minimum collateral requirements no matter how far out of the money the option, this calculation helps you avoid those seemingly no-risk fractional options sales in favor of more substantial ones. It can't be said too often that a strategy of selling fractional option premiums over time can lead to occasional, but very large and unexpected, losses.

As a rule of thumb, you should aim for a 50 to 100 percent annualized profit potential on each trade. By the time you take your losses, pay your commissions, and account for trade slippage, you should come down to a reasonable return for the risk you're running—say, 20 to 35 percent per year.

OPTIONS ARE
OPTIONAL.

For the average investor, they're not worth the risk. Something like 70
percent of all options expire worthless, and they are expensive because of
the time-value premium attached to them. They have a limited time
horizon, which means you're not investing for the long term. And speculating means you're not effectively managing risk. Commodities carry
many of the same features and are potentially ruinous (and by ruinous, I
mean bankruptcy-type ruinous) if done via leverage. But for speculators,
there are certain advantages to options that can't be denied.

PROFITS AND LOSSES—

Nothing Ventured, Nothing Gained

DON'T COUNT YOUR CHICKENS
UNTIL THEY'RE HATCHED.

People will endlessly add up their paper profits. They open a position and when it moves to a profit, they count the profit. "I've made $2,000," they say enough times to believe that they've made that money. It's a potentially deadly mistake.

Throughout 2000 and 2001, stories came to light about many dot.com millionaires who, faced with large paper profits, borrowed against their stock positions to buy large homes, airplanes, and boats. When their stocks cratered and the collateral was insufficient to hold down the notes, the bank or brokerage house called for more collateral. In many cases, stock had to be sold at depressed prices to pay for the hit.

Those investors, as close as they were to their companies, simply could not conceive of an 80 or 90 percent drop in the price of the stock. They confused paper profits with real ones.

You don't have the profit until you close the position. Until then, it's all an illusion, a phantom. Today's paper profit can turn into tomorrow's loss. In an unforgiving market era where it is not uncommon to see stocks crater 50 percent in a morning, surely none of us can count that money until it's in our hand.

Good businesspeople know this. They don't count the sale until they see the cash in their bank account. They know that too many things can go wrong between making the sale and getting paid. So it is in the markets. If you plan your investment strategy predicated on paper profits and unrealized gains, you will, at some point, take on more risk than you should. Whether using that paper gain as collateral for a loan or increasing your risk profile because of a new and larger account size, you need to be extremely cautious.

If you buy ABC Widget at $10 and it moves to $15, you have a $5 profit when you sell the stock and the trade settles. Until then, it's all just so much paper.

THE ONLY RETURN THAT COUNTS
IS THE REAL RETURN.

The *real return* is the amount of money you get to keep over and above the rate of inflation. It's easy to fool yourself into thinking that your returns are higher than they actually are.

Consider a 10 percent short-term capital gain earned in a 3 percent inflation environment:

- First, you have to reduce the return by about 50 percent to account for federal and state income taxes. This leaves a 5 percent after-tax return.

- Then you need to reduce that return by the rate of inflation, which leaves, net, a 2 percent real rate of return.

Two percent doesn't feel nearly as good as 10 percent. All that work for a lousy 2 percent? That's right. And that's why, for many investors, investing isn't about making money, it's really about having an enjoyable hobby. If you want to earn a 2 percent real rate of return, you could probably index your portfolio and sit on the long-term capital gains generated to increase that real rate of return.

That's not as much fun, but for many people, it's probably more profitable.

It's all about getting the odds on your side.

This is such a simple concept that most investors forget to consider it. Yet, as an investor, there are a host of things in your way. Returns are eaten up by bid/ask spreads, taxes, commissions, bad investment choices, selling too soon, buying too late, waiting too long, not having enough patience, getting the flu, and going on vacation. So, over time, all these little things nick away at your success. Each one, experienced once, may not be a big deal. After all, anyone should be able to shut down and go to the beach for a week!

But, over a lifetime, they eat away profits, like termites eating away the wall of a house.

To combat this performance erosion, you need to do everything you can to get the odds on your side. Accumulate a lifetime of little things that help, not hinder, your performance. If you do enough of these little things, you can greatly overcome all those niggling little disasters that eat away at your profits.

For instance, long-term capital gains taxes are one-half the rate of short-term gains. Generally, strive to take long-term gains and cut your taxes by half! If you find commissions an issue because of your activity, try changing your discipline to slow down the number of transactions. If you're an options trader, don't plan your vacation to fall on the third Friday of the month—you'll be forced to close positions rather than wait to see them expire worthless. Commodity traders should pick entry and exit points carefully.

In short, you need to get the odds on your side. Cutting costs, cutting taxes, and careful decision making are all habits to develop.

A LOSS IS A LOSS
IS A LOSS.

Understand what constitutes a loss. Many investors don't feel they actually have a loss as long as they don't sell. But that's not really true. A loss on paper is still a loss. In fact, it's a loss that can grow since you haven't stemmed the bleeding. This refusal to face reality is an excellent example of the role psychology plays in investing.

Selling a stock at a loss means we have to admit we made a mistake. That's painful, but not as painful as missing out on other profits or losing even more.

THE FIRST LOSS
IS THE SMALLEST LOSS.

This investing truism is a key to portfolio management. It's why we sometimes set loss limits on the stocks we hold. It also encourages you to think about liquidating the position.

When you think about it, liquidating with a small loss carries very little financial penalty. Do the math. If you have a $100,000 account, and your short position in XYZ Widgets has moved against you (due to the introduction of the new Aussie Widget, a sports model widget for the outdoor type) to the tune of a $500 loss, taking that loss will have little impact on your portfolio.

You were wrong. You pay your $500 tuition to Mr. Market and get out. If you stay in, one of two things will happen: Either the loss will deepen, or the loss will turn into a profit.

The odds generally favor the loss deepening. This means if you want to find investment positions that will show future losses, look for positions that are currently at a loss or have been eroding in value. Conversely, if you want to find a profitable investment, look to investments that have been increasing in value.

If shorting XYZ has been a loser's game, then the odds are probably better than 50/50 that it will continue to be a loser's game (trends tend to continue). Looking for a turnaround in the position is generally less than a 50/50 proposition.

The second possibility, that the loss deepens, is more likely. A body in motion tends to stay in motion. So when the position is put on and the initial movement shows a loss, you should strongly consider closing out the position and moving on to something else.

But, you say, how much of a loss should move you out? I believe that a 25 percent loss is a reasonable point at which to exit. Less than that may cause you to fall victim to small, noisy swings in price. More than 25 percent signals the likelihood of a bad investment getting worse.

If you take a 3 percent position, and the position moves 25 percent against you, it is an overall loss of 0.75 percent. You can survive a lot of those while simultaneously freeing precious capital to look for better opportunity elsewhere.

Mental loss limits can work for those investors who have the discipline to stick to them. For most of us, I believe mechanical loss limits are better than mental ones, although I recognize that they have their downsides:

- If there is a broad market correction, you run the risk of having a big piece of your portfolio sold off.

- If the stock is volatile, failing to set a wide-enough stop-loss could take you out of the security in the course of its normal daily fluctuation.

Pruning losses demands discipline. The art of taking a loss is among the most difficult to learn in the art of investing. As you can see, even a mechanical stop-loss has its problems. The more you investigate how to take a loss, the more you become aware of the pitfalls. You would think that this would make it all an empty exercise.

But there is a great virtue in all of this. If you study losses long enough, you will find great wisdom in the maxim "The first loss is the smallest loss." You come to realize that since there is no good answer in terms of when to take a loss, there is a good solution in taking small ones.

DON'T MAKE THE
SAME MISTAKE TWICE.

There are also hidden costs of letting losses run. These are *opportunity losses* (losses of potential profits in other stocks because your money was tied up in a loser). Once you monetize a loss, that money can be redeployed into potential winners. In other words, a loss on a stock means, of course, that you have lost capital. But that's not the end of it. The loss is actually greater than that because you could have used the money you invested in stock A (a loser) to buy stock B (a winner). Holding onto a loser is, in essence, making the same mistake twice. No one wants to do that.

DON'T AVERAGE DOWN
ON A LOSER.

It's tempting to take another shot at a stock you believe in, even though it has turned down against you. In some cases, that desire may be correct. But following our approach in which capital preservation is paramount, you likely would have been taken out of a loser with a stop-loss. Generally, you should buy more of a stock only when the second purchase is at a price *higher* than the first. Mr. Market is telling you you're on the right track.

LOSSES ARE THE
MARKET'S TUITION.

The market takes you to school. It teaches you lessons. Sometimes, you learn the hard way. Some lessons are easy and some are hard. From time to time, an investor can be stubborn and refuse to learn. The market will simply send him to the woodshed, extract some more tuition, and try to teach him again.

The market is a great teacher. It is very patient. It will wait and wait and wait some more. It's in no hurry to graduate the current class. It would just as soon keep you in school as long as it can, all the while charging you tuition to learn from your mistakes.

You can't go to market school without paying tuition. Depending on how quick a learner you are, the bill will be large or the bill will be small. You'll pay big once a year or you'll slowly bleed your capital week after week.

No matter. These losses—these lessons—are your tuition. If you are going to attend a great school and graduate, it will be expensive. As a matter of fact, I'm sure that if I added up my tuition, it would far exceed the cost of a first-class undergraduate education. Think of the next loss you take as tuition. It will focus you on learning from the experience instead of merely expressing your anger. Then you will learn.

The market never stops charging you. You never really graduate. As you gather knowledge and grow surer of your technique, your tuition bills will go down. Still, learning in the market is a lifelong experience. It's a university without a degree, without a graduation ceremony. At some point, you'll know when you've arrived, when you understand. Even then, the market will whack you once in a while. Learn from it.

WHEN YOU'VE TAKEN SOME HITS, TRADE SMALL.

In order to speculate successfully, you need to be on an even emotional keel. You need to maximize your ability to think clearly and exercise good judgment. Clear thinking purges negative thoughts and emotions, such as trying to get even, exact revenge, or muscle the market.

If you've had a string of losses, it can't help but upset you, even in small ways. When things aren't going well, it can be frustrating and engender feelings of anger. This isn't the optimal way to trade in the market. What's more, at such times your self-confidence has probably taken a bit of a beating—perhaps a hell of a beating. When your self-confidence is down, it is much more difficult to trade correctly and with good judgment. You begin to doubt your trading style or system, and you tend to overtrade, either by trading more actively or by taking larger positions.

If you feel these emotions catching up with you, there is really only one solution: You need to begin to trade small again. What do I mean by trading small? If your usual position is $10,000 per stock, begin new positions with $5,000 instead. If you typically buy or sell five corn contracts, trade only two. If you usually sell three naked call positions, sell only one.

By trading smaller, you reduce your own fear of failure and anxiety and give yourself some breathing room to get back in the groove again. In effect, these smaller positions are like practice swings to warm you up properly.

The ultimate way to trade smaller is to quit trading for a while. Take a break. In my experience, that is very hard to do, because after a string of losses, we are eager to make those losses back as quickly as we can. As a practical solution, therefore, trading small is probably more attainable than quitting for a while.

Once your smaller trading begins to show profits, your self-confidence and self-esteem will rise along with your profit profile. Then, *and only then*, should you move back to more normal positions.

One caveat: If you are a systems trader and have run into a string of losses, the proper way to trade is to continue trading according to your system. It is Gallea's first law of systems trading: Once you stop trading your system, it would have worked superbly had you continued. The market conditions that caused your system to stop working were, no doubt, temporary and will be followed by conditions allowing for excellent profit opportunity.

Nonetheless, you need to be gentle with yourself. When things have been bad and you're feeling low, reduce your positions and get back on a more even keel. Just keep practicing those warm-up swings until you start hitting the ball again. It does wonders for your batting average.

GATHER
YOUR DEAD.

Do postmortems on all your trades. What did you do right? What did you do wrong? Look at your winners. What could you have done better? Where could you have improved your technique? What influences caused you to buy and to sell? Were they correct? Did you ignore relevant data? Did you act emotionally and not rationally? Did you pay attention to your risk rules and not violate them?

After looking at your winners, look at your losses. What caused the loss? Was it a bad investment from the start, or did it deteriorate? Did you sell too soon or too late? Ask the same questions about your losers that you did about your winners: risk rules, relevant data, and so on.

Over the years, I found that by doing this, I was doing the same thing a golf pro does when he videotapes your golf swing. He replays the action and looks for flaws, he then goes in and corrects your mistakes, and, eventually, your swing gets better. It's not easy to do this. We'd all prefer to quickly move on and buy another winner, to make up for a loser. But the best time we can spend is looking at our past actions, replaying them in slow motion.

By doing this, I discovered that I tended to be early in my purchases—often months early. Knowing that taught me to delay a purchase once I had put together an investment thesis. For instance, a particular stock would collapse, and (being a contrarian by nature) I could often put together a rationale for why the stock should go back up. But while I was focused on the future turnaround, Mr. Market would decide the stock had to spend some time as dead money or a head fake with additional losses ahead before a bottom. There was a timing disconnect in my thinking. Now I haven't entirely solved the problem and, truth be told, might never. The market isn't that easy to figure out, but I do tend to keep my left arm straight more often, and I don't lift up my head as much either.

Start today. Look at this year's closed trades and analyze them. Play 'em back in slow motion. See how your head moves? See how you sway when you bring the club back? See how you rush your swing? See what you learn. You'll be surprised by what you see.

PSYCHOLOGY—

It's All in Your Head

KNOW YOURSELF.

Anytime potential clients sit with us to discuss our services, we always ask about their tolerance for risk. Since so many people have difficulty with the question, we frame it in terms of a dollar loss to the portfolio (a percentage loss is too abstract and unreal).

"Mr. Jones, if you were to lose $200,000 of your $1,000,000 portfolio, how would you feel about that? Would that be an acceptable loss?"

As often as not, the person's first answer is the wrong one. People seem to want to avoid appearing wimpy or weak, so they admit to a larger tolerance for risk than is actually the case. When we probe the first answer ("Now, you say you would be willing to risk $200,000 in a market decline. Are you sure?"), about three-quarters of the time, the individual changes his or her mind.

This has taught me that people aren't entirely honest about, or completely aware of, their tolerance for risk. This, in turn, causes many people to take greater risks than they should, which naturally leads to them bailing out of the markets (a flight response to the fear they feel).

Just as with other aspects of investing, emotions play a big role in whether or not the methodology you choose will work. Knowing that your emotions often lead you in the wrong direction should help minimize the negative effects of an emotional reaction to market events. Ideally, of course, your emotions should never be allowed into the game. A good starting point is to accurately judge your tolerance for risk. By not testing yourself beyond your tolerance, you keep fear out of the game, which can only benefit your work.

THE MARKET MOVES
IN YOUR MIND.

Look at any stock or index chart. What do you see? However drawn (point and figure, bar, candlestick, etc.), the chart shows you recent trading history as a series of data points. The lines on the chart will not change, no matter how long you look at them. They are the same for all observers.

However, forecasting where the market moves, where the chart will move, is all in your own mind. It is an interpretation that you make based on those lines. If you are inclined to be bullish, and the market has been trending higher, you will tend to imagine a continuation of that trend. If the market has been going down, you will see bottoms that don't exist.

If you're bearish, you'll see the opposite. If the market has been rising, you see tops that don't exist, and if the market has been going down, you'll see a continuation of that trend.

Investors fool themselves if they think they are analyzing a chart with an objective point of view. The market moves in your mind. You create a future scenario that you hope is objective, but you have to allow for the fact that it might also be wishful thinking. It's a thin straw upon which to risk your financial future. It's another good reason to make small bets and not bet the ranch.

ACT IN THE
FACE OF FEAR.

Make no mistake about it. All traders, all investors face fear. Even the most expert have their moments with it. You can never entirely eliminate the feeling, no matter how much time you work in the markets.

However, it is equally true that one of the attributes that separates the accomplished investor from the rank amateur is that the accomplished investor is able to act in the face of fear, in spite of that fear.

It stands to reason that if you want to maximize your profits, you want to buy low and sell high. This means that when the markets go into free-fall, when prices are being marked down in a wholesale and unreasoning way, you want to be a buyer. Of course, this is also the time of maximum fear. All investors will hesitate in such an environment. But some will act in spite of their emotions, while most will be paralyzed by it.

These are the moments of maximum potential for your portfolio. These are the times when very few are willing to step up to the plate and buy. As a result, the majority (those selling) must sell at a much lower price to entice the minority (those willing to buy) to do so. The market, being a risk-transference mechanism, pays the most to the buyer in that situation (by giving him a cheap price at which to buy), because the buyer is taking on a lot of risk and needs to be compensated for it.

Being afraid is perfectly acceptable. It happens to everyone. But it is in working in the face of fear and panic that opportunity is found.

WHEN YOU LOSE YOUR COURAGE, BACK OFF.

We all have periods of time when we are uncertain about what to do. Usually this loss of confidence is the result of having experienced a string of losses. When this happens, the natural tendency is to push harder, to put on larger or more frequent trades to make up for those losses. This is the exact opposite of what you should do.

To regain your confidence, which is crucial for successful investing, you need to reduce the size of your positions on new trades. For example, if you normally take a $20,000 bite, reduce the size to $5,000. If your usual trade is five option contracts, trade two or even one.

Reducing the size of your trades will help you relax. It lowers anxiety and allows rational thought to come through, and lets you reestablish your system and methodology. Once you have grounded yourself again, once you are again comfortable with your trading, you can increase the size of your trades to previous levels.

A final thought: Be sure you go back and analyze what happened. You want to know what you did wrong.

MAKE DECISIONS RATIONALLY,
NOT EMOTIONALLY.

When we put our capital at risk, we fall prey to two conflicting emotions: fear and greed. On the one hand, we fear losing our money. Simultaneously, we are greedy to earn more. These are two powerful emotions, and since the two are in constant conflict, the impact that has on the investor should not be underestimated. And the greater the fear/greed factor, the more pronounced the effort to take emotion out of it must be. You'll never eliminate emotion; you can only mitigate its effects.

The fear/greed factor is most pronounced in commodity trading, where risk is highest. It is, therefore, not surprising that so many methods for trading futures are mechanical in nature. If you religiously follow a mechanical system, you've taken all of the emotion out of it.

In its least emotional form, you would settle on the system and then turn it over to someone else to follow. Presumably, since it's not that person's money, she would follow your system to the letter. Of course, this takes the fun out of the exercise. Another emotion—pleasure—is also at work.

The point is that in a very high risk environment (futures) mechanical systems are numerous. And in a low-risk environment such as fixed income, systems are absent.

This is an important lesson. You must trade and invest based on reason, not on emotion. Emotions are notoriously unstable and misleading. They are characterized by temporary chemical imbalances of the brain, heightened physical responses, and temporary loss of your ability to reason—in short, the same things you'd see in a teenager in love.

The next time you're about to pull the trigger in an emotional response to events, think about your daughter's boyfriend. That should give you pause for reflection.

"THINGS ARE NOT
DIFFERENT THIS TIME."

Sometimes, things are different. Maybe a stock has had two or three false starts. Everyone anticipated a change in the earnings outlook, only to be disappointed. Then, when the change takes hold, someone will say, "Things are different this time," and things do indeed turn out to be different. Most people in that situation will miss the move, however. The result: a conversion to the "things are different this time" philosophy.

Unfortunately, most of the time when someone tries to make a case that reason won't allow, the commentator falls back on the "things are different this time" defense to make the point. Most of the time, this argument fails. Things are definitely *not* different almost all of the time.

There is no more vivid example than the Internet mania of 1999. Earnings didn't matter any more (things are different this time), tangible product didn't matter any more (things are different this time), conventional measures of value such as free cash flow didn't matter any more (things are different this time). Of course, things weren't different and most e-concepts hit the runway without wheels down.

The fact of the matter is that very little changes in the basic nature of the markets, because very little changes in human beings and how they behave. Fear and greed still drive the market, and whether lusting after Radio Corporation of America in 1929 or bowing at the feet of dot.com fever in 1999, it's all the same kettle of fish. Just as people could buy RCA in 1929 believing that it would grow infinitely, their heirs would draw the very same conclusions 70 years later about companies that existed only in cyberspace.

Just as RCA pushed its product out in endless invisible packets of information across space, so did dot.coms push theirs in equally invisible packets of information across a more modern space. And even as they were following a business plan written nearly a century ago, the true believers proclaimed, "It's different this time."

I've learned that the more people proclaim, "It's different this time," the more likely it is that we're about to repeat some market excess from the past.

IGNORE THE BUZZING
MOSQUITOES.

Most of what you hear every day about the markets is noise. It's like a gaggle of mosquitoes buzzing around your head all day—it gets your attention. It can be satisfying when you swat one, and it can be irritating when you get bit. But, in the overall scheme of your life, it's a non-event.

So it is in the markets. If you're a consumer of financial news (and I'm the worst of the news junkies), you're going to be surrounded by mosquitoes. On a quiet day in August, an earnings warning from a company you've never heard of, and may never hear of again, gets front and center attention. On a slow morning in February, some minor economic statistic will be parsed and played over and over again—like mosquitoes buzzing around your head.

All the while you're swatting and whacking, you're sitting on a portfolio of investments—positions that you've carefully entered after long and arduous research—equities that you intend to own for years, nay, decades! Then, after one too many kamikaze attacks at your head, in a frustration-driven frenzy, you sell something.

You've got to be able to develop the ability to separate the important from the trivial. Just because something gets a lot of airtime or a lot of ink doesn't make it important.

THE PLEASURE PRINCIPLE: YOU'RE PAID IN PLEASURE OR PROFIT.

We can't underestimate the pleasure/entertainment factor in the invest-ment equation. You would think that people are only interested in profit, but the fact is that they're also interested in having fun.

At first blush, you would equate pleasure with profit. It's fun to make money, so you would assume that the profit motive is the core of the pleasure to be gained from investing. Surprisingly, this isn't neces-sarily true.

For most investors, hard work isn't fun. Hard work entails reading the footnotes, investigating the accounting practices, analyzing the industry. It means looking at crop reports, reserves for loan losses, or 100 other things, depending on the vehicle. That's hard work, though it pays off if you do enough of it.

Now, some investments have very little potential for investment return, but they are a lot of fun to own (until the losses hit). Penny stocks are an example. Buying 100,000 shares of a 10-cent stock, you buy end-less dreams and visions of wealth. Contrast that to a position in a beaten-down aluminum stock. Frankly, there isn't a lot of fun in tracking aluminum stocks, but there can be a lot of profit in doing so.

As an investor, you have a choice. You can invest for profit or you can invest for fun. If you protest that you're really in it for the profit and not the fun, go back and look at your portfolio. Illuminating, isn't it?

THERE ARE OLD TRADERS AND THERE ARE BOLD TRADERS, BUT THERE AREN'T ANY OLD, BOLD TRADERS.

If you get a chance, visit the trading floor of a broker-dealer. You especially want to visit its NASDAQ area, where some of the high-octane stuff changes hands.

Typically, you'll see row on row of very bright, energetic, intense people, all peering intently into flashing screens. Some chew gum to work off the tension; others squeeze a tennis ball; still others rock back and forth. You don't have to ask them about stress. You can see it.

The thing that will strike you is the age of the traders. Almost without exception, they're under 40 years old; a lot of them are under 30. It's been that way as long as I've been in the business. Young people. I've often wondered what happened to the young people I saw in 1981 or the class from 1985 or 1990. If people could stick it out, you'd expect to see some grandparents, some middle-aged paunches, and an occasional 40th birthday party.

It's a tough profession. It's like war. The machine that is the market chews them up and spits them out. To be a trader, you need to be bold—not reckless, because it's the house's money you're putting at risk—and you need to be decisive and quick.

As I said, as you wander around the floor, you see a lot of bold traders. But you don't see old traders. The old traders trade somewhere else, where the pace isn't so quick, where reflexes can slow a bit. They're off the floor; maybe they've moved over to the relative quiet of the corporate bond desk.

Think about how the market runs people through the meat grinder. You, too, can be bold or you can continue until you're old, but you probably can't get to be both old and bold.

SMART INVESTORS
THINK THEY KNOW VERY LITTLE.

As I accumulate more and more experience in the markets, I notice a completely unexpected phenomenon. Instead of having more answers, I seem to develop more questions. Now, it's not because I'm not learning. Goodness knows, Mr. Market has taken enough tuition from me. But even as my technique improves, I seem to be more willing to seek answers than offer them.

As I noticed this in myself, I began to see other market participants differently. From time to time, I recognize this same attribute in others, often in private conversations with successful investors. The conversations would be peppered with phrases such as "I had a lot of luck," "I was fortunate," and "in spite of myself."

Conversely, I noticed that many people new to investing seemed to be sure of their answers and had very little in the way of questions (I can always tell where we are in the market by whether people have a question for me or, instead, offer me unsolicited advice).

It finally dawned on me that people who really do understand the market have come to that knowledge the hard way. They have faced the fire of the market and the heartbreak it can dish out in its own heartless way. They've come through the crucible of fire and out the other side. They have the wary and grateful attitude of the survivor.

Ever listen to a survivor of a natural disaster?

"I was fortunate."

"I had a lot of luck."

"In spite of myself . . ."

Same thing.

TAKE TIME OFF.

Whether you are trading, speculating, or investing, there is a tremendous emotional and energy-draining aspect to putting money at risk. And when you do it, day after day, there is an accumulation of stress that can't be avoided and can't be denied.

We all recognize that when losses occur, stress rises and we need a break. What isn't as obvious is the stress of accumulating winners. We assume that because winning is fun, it doesn't carry stress. Of course, it is true that losing is the more stressful of the two, but handling winning has its problems. For one thing, you've got the stress of letting the profit get away, which causes its share of nail biting and fingers thrumming on the desk.

Eventually, enough of this stuff builds up and you begin to lose perspective. This leads to a loss of good judgment. A highly disciplined trading/investing system is great because it can help you stay on track when you do lose perspective, but I've found that once I lose perspective, I have difficulty following my system, which leads to a tendency to wing it. Shooting from the hip isn't a good idea.

Now, you're not going to go out and murder people because your trading has increased your stress level, and in all probability, you'll still be able to pet the dog and scratch the cat. But this loss of perspective and the resulting loss of good judgment make a very dangerous state of mind. It is all too easy to pull the trigger on a trade and create a real problem.

Every once in a while, you need to just shut it down and walk away for a bit. I think the best time to do that is after a winning streak. It is also the worst time to try it because you're brimming with enthusiasm and want to continue. Nevertheless, I can assure you that this is correct trading strategy, especially because systems and techniques go in and out of favor, and you're probably due for a draw down anyway. If, for example, you've been using a trend-following system with great success, it's likely that the market will enter a trading range in which your trend-following system will accrue losses.

One of the great benefits of investing in the markets is that you have liquidity. You can shut the thing down and go away for a week. We all need to do that.

How do you know you need a break? It's easy. You'll just know it. You'll find yourself telling yourself, "I need a vacation."

THINK LIKE
A ROOKIE.

One habit I've developed over the years is to try and put myself in the place of a novice investor. I ask myself, "What would a rookie do here?"

It's a trick I use when I'm confused. I may be unsure about what I should do, but having been a novice (we all were at one time), I know what I used to do. As a rule, I usually can be a lot more certain of what a rookie *would* do than what I *should* do. Once I've figured out what a rookie would do, I consider doing the opposite.

Here's a simple example: You're watching your favorite business channel, and you hear a breathless story about how XYZ is soaring on rumors of the introduction of a new product. It's just a rumor, and the stock is cheap. The stock has moved from $4.00 to $5.50 on heavy volume. It was trading at $3.00 the week before. Should you buy the stock?

I know, absolutely, what the novice is going to do. The novice is going to buy the stock. To find out if that is indeed the case, I check the trade-by-trade detail, and, sure enough, I find hundreds of trades in the 100-to-1,000–share range. That tells me that institutional buying isn't moving that stock higher. (I also know that most institutions won't buy a stock priced at less than $5.00.)

Now, my decision is easy. I won't touch the stock. I won't buy it, because I don't want to play on the same side of the line as emotional buyers. I won't sell it short either, because if the rumor is true, I'd be on the wrong side of a cheap stock that can only get pushed higher. Just as important, even if I'm right and the stock goes down, I can only make a dollar or two, so in order to make the trade count, I need to short a lot of stock. Doing so would expose me to a large adverse move. It just isn't worth it.

A little bit of careful thinking can go a long way in these situations. And thinking like a rookie is often the best thinking you can do.

TAKE PERSONAL RESPONSIBILITY
FOR YOUR RESULTS.

There comes a time when you feel victimized.

You will have a bad fill or a poor execution, or you'll buy a stock that doesn't work out. You will find yourself blaming the market, the market makers, the locals in Chicago, or the analyst who recommended the stock. Maybe the Internet failed and you couldn't get the trade off, or perhaps it was the pressure your boss put on you that kept you from thinking clearly.

It is inevitable that we will take out our frustrations on others. We've all done it. In many human endeavors, doing that can be relatively harmless. If you drop a fly ball because the sun was in your eyes, it usually doesn't cause any harm to curse at the sun.

But when investing, the unwillingness to take personal responsibility for investing results can be fatal. Let's be clear: Every time you pull the trigger to buy or to sell, you are exercising your own free will to do so. No one is forcing you to make that trade. You are under no court edict ordering you to do so. Your friends could care less. All in all, it's your call and you make the decision.

It could very well be true that your computer froze and you couldn't get the trade off. Or maybe the analyst really blew the call. Absolutely. But it was your decision to enter into a strategy that required access to the market at all times. It was your decision to listen to that analyst. No matter how well founded your complaint, in the end it was your call to make and, ultimately, your mistake.

Once I began to take complete responsibility for my investing, investing became more fun and I think (but can't prove) that it improved my technique. You see, if you come to know that you are indeed in control, it is much easier to correct what's wrong. No longer a victim of the fates and the furies, you realize that you are the solution to the problem and that, with enough work, you can fix it.

This is a liberating thought. It frees you from fear and puts you in a positive, problem-solving frame of mind. Instead of blaming the computer, which will no doubt fail you again, you set about liberating yourself from dependence on it. Maybe you buy a second one. Perhaps you abandon a strategy that demands 100 percent flawless access.

Whatever your solution, taking complete responsibility cuts two ways. When your results sparkle, you'll enjoy them that much more.

DON'T UNDERESTIMATE
NON-EVENT FEEDBACK.

Non-event feedback occurs when you do something wrong but don't pay a price for it—your mistake is a non-event. You proceed on, blissfully unaware that it's only a matter of time before your mistake jumps out and grabs you by the throat.

Consider the investor who loads up on a single investment. Perhaps she buys an out-of-the-money, 60-day option for 20 cents per contract. An unexpected takeover rockets the stock and she pockets a 500 percent profit. Flush with success, she finds another stock and the same thing happens.

Now this investor is doubly cursed. First, she's engaging in a trading strategy that has a very low probability of long-term profit. If she's going to buy high-risk options, she should do so with a small fraction of her capital. Or, if she's going to risk all of her capital, she needs to be very conservative about the way in which she does it.

The second curse is that she's unaware of her stupidity. She's getting non-event feedback. Worse, she's getting positive feedback. In short, she's making mistake after mistake and doesn't know it.

Of course, the third time she does it, the stock sits like a stone, the options erode to zero, and she's got a 100 percent loss. It doesn't matter that she had two 500-percent wins. By rolling the dice a third time, she rolled all those wins up into the third toss, and she lost.

There is a lesson here. You can do something wrong and receive non-event feedback or even positive feedback for doing it. Just because what you are doing results in a win doesn't mean it was right. It's often luck. Analyze your winners just as hard as your losers. Make sure that your victory was earned and not simply luck.

The problem with non-event feedback is that it's, well, a non-event. That's why it is so insidious and dangerous.

YOU CAN'T ESCAPE
THE HARD DECISION.

Sometimes we play mental gymnastics with ourselves in order to escape a tough decision. We think that if we can just reason it out a bit more, look at the numbers more closely, or find another factor to analyze, we can find the key to the lock that will let us make the right call on a tough question.

I gave a speech one night to a group of accountants employed by industrial firms and members of the Institute for Management Accountants. After the speech, we had time for the usual Q&A. The first question concerned a local company and whether or not it should be bought, sold, or held. The company had produced six years of stellar returns. Earnings and sales increased year after year like clockwork—about 28 percent per year. The stock split three for two each year, again just like clockwork. With current year's earnings of 56 cents per share and a price of $57 per share, the company was carrying a P/E ratio of 100. Buy, sell, or hold? Here is what I said:

"As long as the company can continue to make its numbers, can continue to show that very steady growth rate, it can continue to go up. Now, you should know that since it's trading at over three times its growth rate, it is priced to that perfection. The first time it misses its numbers, even by a penny, the stock will probably get cut in half. So you have a simple decision to make. Do you run the risk of it missing a number, or do you hold, believing that it will make its numbers?"

It all boiled down to that. You could study the company's financials for a very long time and conclude that everything was fine. But it all came down to that quarterly earnings number. And no matter how much you studied the situation, you couldn't escape the fact that it was all an unknown. Hit the numbers and all is well. Miss a number and look out below.

It is my guess that a few people might have sold a bit of stock out of nervousness, but I would also guess that most of them continued to hold it, even though they knew that the ax was never far away.

Sometimes you just can't escape a tough decision.

WHEN THE NEWS IS BAD,
BE A CRITICAL READER.

I've noticed that when a company gets in trouble, a feeding frenzy of pessimism can overwhelm events. The frenzy is everywhere—the media, the analysts, and the investing public.

It's hard to know, in advance, what circumstances create this bad news, so you can't anticipate it. At times, it seems that people just get angry. It almost always seems to revolve around a management that hasn't delivered. Maybe they promised the moon and didn't deliver it. Maybe they promised a turnaround and didn't deliver. Sometimes people simply lose patience.

Whatever the cause, you can tell there's a frenzy of pessimism because all the articles and reports you read seem to have two outstanding characteristics: First, they are unbelievably gloomy. Second, and perhaps more illuminating, the writer has taken the time to interview customers or suppliers to drive in the knife.

You've seen it before. A company has a bad quarter, the stock plummets, management wrings its hands. Then the kicker comes. Customers who have anecdotal experience about how lousy it all is are interviewed: "I've been a loyal customer of ABC Widgets since 1962 and I couldn't believe it when they pulled my Widget Recycler out of my plant because the salesman didn't know who I was!" That kind of thing.

I always pay more attention when they start interviewing the customers. I've found that it's not a bad signal as a contrarian indicator. When the customers go on record about how bad a company is, improvement is sometimes just around the corner. CEOs just can't stand to be humiliated like that in public.

THINK FOR YOURSELF.

One of the biggest differences between a good investor and a rank amateur is that the good investor is capable of taking in the facts and reaching her own conclusion. She does not parrot what she reads or hears. Rather, she distills the facts and constructs a conclusion from scratch.

Most investors have neither the courage of their convictions nor the complete trust in their own judgment to act independently. They feel that others know more, so they tend to look for other opinions and act on them. The consummate investor cares only about the opinions of others insofar as it helps her discern how others will act and how those actions will drive markets.

It took me a very long time to get to that place. I'm not sure how it happened. I believe it slowly creeps up on you until, one day, you find yourself throwing off a blanket. For me, it was a liberating experience. I reached the point where I believed that I had paid my dues, had accumulated enough experience, and had worked hard enough, so that my opinion was as valid as anyone else's.

At that point, I was able to analyze and reach conclusions independent of the analysis of others. It didn't mean that I disagreed with them all the time; it didn't mean that I felt superior to their work. I still read the analysis and listen to the opinions of others. The difference is that I now feel better able to sift the wheat from the chaff, to retain what I believe is important, and to mentally discard what I think isn't.

This is an important goal to work toward. You want to achieve that feeling of competence and the comfort of exercising a sure hand. You're still going to make mistakes, but you will find yourself more often in a state of calm than in a state of anxiety or flux about your decisions. When you are calm, reason can work its way and your results will inevitably improve.

RISK—

Its Own Reward

IT TAKES GUTS
TO BUY BELLIES.

I have a confession. I love the futures market. I don't mean that I like the futures market, or that I have a fondness for it, or that I find the futures market interesting. I mean that I *love* the futures market.

It's not just the potential for profit. It's also the entire atmosphere that surrounds it. There is the silly humor about getting 5,000 bushels of corn delivered on my lawn or what to do with 15,000 pounds of frozen orange juice concentrate. But it's also the speed and the excitement of it.

But it's not time alone that you need to trade commodities. Nor is it a successful system. If you buy/sell four-week breakouts, keep your positions small, and use the stop-loss technique, you're most of the way there.

No, time and a good system aren't all. You also need guts. You need courage. You've got to be able to handle the volatility and the wrenching moves that deplete capital. One of the things you have to get used to, if you use a system, is that a great month is almost always followed closely by a bad month. Things like that sap your energy, perspective, and courage.

This should not be surprising. Any situation high in fear and anxiety will do that. Just imagine trying to get away from a charging rhino that runs a tad faster than you—you'll get the idea. Even as your heart leaps out of your chest and you pump 180 times a minute, you're wondering if he'll tire first or reach you first.

My best advice then is this: If you want to trade commodities, by all means do so. Trade your system faithfully. And if you sense your courage abating, if you sense your gut churning, bag it.

Test your tolerance;
set your limits.

The history of modern capital markets shows that bear market declines of 20 percent or more are fairly common. If you invest over a lifetime of asset accumulation, you're going to see a number of nasty market breaks, and declines plus an occasional market panic or crash. We often forget about this fact of market life.

When advising new clients about risk, I have them role-play a scenario. It goes something like this:

Let's assume that we put all of your money into the market tomorrow morning—all in common stocks. Whether we use a group of money managers or index funds, or we do it ourselves, we'll also assume that we buy good-quality stocks and we are well diversified. The economy begins to weaken, and over the next year, your $500,000 portfolio drops in value to $400,000—a 20 percent decline.

Since I'm your advisor, you'll come into see me about this, express your concern, and ask what we are going to do about it. And I am going to tell you that we own good stocks (or have good managers or own good funds) and that over long periods of time the stock market has returned about 10 to 12 percent per year. My advice: We should simply take the pain and stay the course.

The question is, what would *you* do?

Would you fire me? Would you fire the manager(s)? Would you sell out and go to cash? Or would you stick to the game plan and bear the pain?

It's an illuminating exercise, because in four out of five cases, the client elects to take on less risk. They realize that the truth of the matter is that they're not willing to risk 20 percent of their money for a long-run return of 10 to 12 percent; therefore, they throttle it back.

If four out of five of our clients do so, then I would guess that four out of five readers of this book are probably taking more risk than they should. What's more, the odds are pretty good that you're one of the four.

FIRST FOCUS ON RISK, THEN ON RETURN.

If there is only one lesson you take away from this book, this should be it.

This is very hard for many people to understand and I think it leads to most of the really bad things that happen in the markets. Whether it is the commodity speculator wiped out, the small stock player decimated, or the large institutional portfolio riddled, the story is almost always the same: too much risk taken on a poor idea.

It's not a poor concept that sinks a ship. Everyone has them. Goodness knows that 20 years in the markets have given me ample opportunity to have had bad ideas in abundance. It's that big "sure thing" position that backfires and gives you a crippling loss. It's loading up on a stock, looking for the big move to take you home, only to have it crater overnight on an unanticipated earnings warning. It's doubling, then tripling up on a winning futures position, only to watch it reverse itself and go limit down for days. It's stubbornly throwing money after money in losing long options positions. All of these behaviors are rooted in greed and can be fatal.

Over 20 years, I've learned a few rules of thumb that help control this tendency:

1. In the futures market, don't risk more than 2 percent of your capital on any single idea.

2. Don't invest more than 3 percent of your capital in any single stock.

3. Don't invest more than 15 percent of your capital in any single industry (all stocks in a single industry tend to move together).

4. Assume your stock portfolio takes a 20 percent hit (a fairly common occurrence in the stock market so far in this century). Compute your losses. Are they bearable?

5. Don't commit more than 10 percent of your capital to purchasing options.

6. When selling naked options, assume that the underlying stock moves three times further than you anticipate. Is the loss bearable?

7. Don't invest all of your money in one asset class (for example, large-cap U.S. stocks, international stocks, futures). Stocks in a class tend to move in the same direction.

8. For the same reason, if you have to own a lot of stock in your employer, then be sure that your other investments have little to do with that stock/industry/market/situation.

9. Try to choose investments that don't correlate highly with each other.

10. Don't speculate with money that you need to pay your living expenses.

If you can follow these rules, you've begun the process of bulletproofing your portfolio. A bulletproof portfolio will survive those periodic firestorms that envelop the markets. You can then develop a long-term outlook, where good investment strategy finds reward.

Never mind about the return. If you are reasonable in your investment selection, the returns will come. But returns only come when you have capital invested. Without capital, you have nothing.

Focus on risk, and prosper.

ORDER
A SALAD.

Be cautious about correlation. Investments don't move in a vacuum. Much like the population of the Amazon jungle or the Pacific Ocean, everything tends to be interconnected.

In terms of investing, correlation is a very important concept. Correlation (the relationship between two different investments) is a subject fit for a book. However, what we can tell you is that you do want to get into a correlation habit. Open an Excel spreadsheet. You'll find that there is a function labeled CORREL. The formula is =COR-REL(array1,array2). Try this: Put the annual returns for the past 10 years of the S&P 500 and the Dow Jones Industrial Average in two separate columns (the S&P in A1:A10 and the Dow in B1:B10). Then, in a blank cell, enter the formula

=CORREL(A1:A10,B1:B10)

See what you get. To make your life simple, here are the numbers you need:

	DOW JONES	S&P 500 INDEX	EAFE
Dec-00	−4.70%	−9.10%	−14.20%
Dec-99	27.30%	21.00%	27.00%
Dec-98	18.20%	28.60%	20.00%
Dec-97	24.90%	33.40%	1.80%
Dec-96	28.90%	23.00%	6.10%
Dec-95	36.90%	37.60%	11.20%
Dec-94	5.00%	1.30%	7.80%
Dec-93	17.00%	10.10%	32.60%
Dec-92	7.40%	7.80%	−12.20%
Dec-91	24.30%	30.60%	12.10%
Dec-90	−0.50%	−3.20%	−23.40%

Perfect correlation is 1.00, which means that the Dow and the S&P move together at the same time, in the same way, like the two rear wheels of your car when you're tooling down the highway. You can see that the Dow and the S&P have a high correlation to each other. If they always moved in opposite directions, the correlation would be negative 1.00; if they moved randomly to each other, 0.50. As you get closer to 1.00, the correlation is stronger, and as you move toward –1.00, the correlation becomes weaker and then completely negative.

Now, in cells C1:C10, enter the annual returns for the Morgan Stanley EAFE (Europe, Australasian, Far East) index and run the correlation function of the EAFE against the Dow or the S&P. Different, isn't it? Can you see how the EAFE (international stocks) doesn't march in lockstep with the other two indexes? Now look at each row. Can you see how sometimes the S&P is up while the EAFE is down and so forth? Go ahead, pretend you have 50 percent S&P and 50 percent EAFE in your portfolio. Average the two together for each year and see what you get.

Can you see how having the two dampens down both risk and reward? Since they don't move together all the time, sometimes one can help the other.

That is the magic of noncorrelation. It turns out that when you properly mix together risky but noncorrelated assets, you can decrease your risk in a meaningful way, but you don't give up the return that the risk reduction would indicate. It is the closest thing to a free lunch in investing that you'll find.

So when you invest, make it a salad. Mix it up—large cap, small cap, international, bonds, cash, metals, REITs. Go ahead. Have a ball. Make a big noncorrelated salad.

DON'T INVEST MORE THAN
15 PERCENT OF YOUR MONEY
IN ANY SINGLE INDUSTRY.

This is an excellent risk control device to limit losses in related stocks.

Many investors are fooled into thinking that owning several stocks in one industry limits the risk of a large industry position. For instance, they want 50 percent of their money in energy stocks or semiconductors, so they buy 10 different energy stocks or 6 different chip stocks. They are lulled into thinking that because they've limited the risk of any single stock, they've reduced portfolio risk.

First, I could easily argue that by buying several stocks, the chance of having a stock blow up completely is also increased. That is, if you own 10 energy stocks, the odds of a stock blowing up have increased tenfold over simply owning one. In addition, by owning a bunch, you've almost certainly reduced the quality of your portfolio, since you now own much more than just the industry leader.

But the real risk you've picked up is the industry risk. If you own six semiconductor stocks, you will find that they all tend to trade on the prospects for the industry and they all move in relatively tight lockstep. Sure, one or two will be better positioned than the others and this will give you a performance boost. But it is also true that you might have one or two more poorly positioned ones and thus a performance dead heat.

Certainly, though, if the industry heads into the tank, you're going to be pulled in underwater because you've tied yourself to it with a big, strong rope. This is why you want to limit an industry exposure to 15 percent. It allows for diversification into at least six industries, and that can provide real risk reduction benefit.

A closing caveat: Several industries make a sector, and you need to be aware that if you have 15 percent each in semiconductors and computer manufacturers, you've now got 30 percent in technology and you begin to pick up the risk of the technology sector.

As you can see, judging your risk can be a bit complicated, so just remember to keep these rules in mind. You may not always create the best mix for risk reduction, but you'll be constantly striving in that direction and that will serve you well over time.

Just do it.

How often have you read the advice that you should dollar-cost average your way into your investments? People advise this because it appears to lower risk. By taking your time to get fully invested, you reduce the chance of buying at the top. By averaging in, using a fixed dollar amount, you can buy more shares at lower prices if the market falls, and if the market rises, you'll have a profit on everything you've bought. This all seems logical enough, but there is a big hidden cost in this strategy.

The fact of the matter is that on average, the market goes up. Historically, the market has gone up about 75 percent of the time. This means that if you dollar-cost average into the market, the odds are three in four that you'll pay a higher price for your investment than if you simply buy it all at once. Therefore, strictly from a cost-acquisition standpoint, dollar-cost averaging is not a proper technique for establishing a market position.

If this is so, then why do people do it? The reason is quite simple: Many people, when they must do something, want to ease into it slowly, to accustom themselves to the risk. If you find yourself thinking about dollar-cost averaging, you are really expressing a fear of loss. You instinctively feel that the position you are about to take is too risky, that if the market goes against you immediately, you'll find yourself in a bad way, with losses above your tolerance.

Such a feeling should act like a splash of cold water, a signal that what you are doing isn't appropriate for your portfolio. Think about it. At some point in the not too distant future, you will be fully invested, averaged in or not. If the level of the risk made you hesitant to put all of your money in at once, then perhaps you're about to take too much overall risk and you should pare it all back.

AS THE MARKET MOVES
IN YOUR FAVOR, BUILD ON IT.

Most investors tend to buy more of a long position as the investment *drops* in value. They should be buying more as it *rises* in value. While at first blush, it may make little sense to pay more and more as you go, a little reflection will show the wisdom of this strategy.

When you build a long position, you are buying an investment that you want to rise in price. (Right? You don't have to be a wizard to know this.) And I think it's safe to assume that you believe the position can go up at least 20 percent, probably 50 to 100 percent. Otherwise, you wouldn't take the risk. That means that if you're right, the investment will indeed rise 50 percent, and you'll have a lot of opportunity to buy more and profit from each piece that you've accumulated.

Therefore, buying more as the price rises means that you're increasing your risk and potential profit as the investment is validating your opinion. If you buy more as the price drops, thinking to lower your cost basis, then you're buying more even as you're being proved wrong. You're doing it, no doubt, because you still think you're right; perhaps your timing was off a bit? If you're right, you're right, and you should wait for a higher price.

At one point, I became bullish on the silver market. I wanted to establish a 10-contract position, controlling 50,000 ounces of silver. I had a $2.00 per ounce profit target and wanted to make $100,000 on the position. I purchased two contracts at $5.00 per ounce. I then set buy-stops at $5.06, $5.12, $5.18, and $5.25 per ounce, two contracts each. Of course, it seems inevitable that as soon as I put on a futures position, the position goes against me. (This is one of Gallea's immutable laws of the market: When he establishes a position, it goes against him.) Silver dropped to $4.90 per ounce. I did not buy more.

Eventually, it went as low as $4.85, but that 15-cent loss on 15,000 ounces was $2,250, well below the risk I could afford on the silver position. Eventually, silver rose, and I bought in more at $5.06 and $5.12. Thus, my average cost at $5.12 was $5.06 on 30,000 ounces. I then set a stop-loss at $4.92 on the entire position. The position went up a couple of cents more and then came down hard, and I was taken out at $4.92. My loss was $3,200.

"Not very successful," you say, and you're right. But consider what happened. I risked about $3,000 for a potential profit of $100,000. That is an excellent risk/reward ratio of 33 to 1. But I would have lost less if I had bought more as it went down. Right?

Consider this. Let's say that after buying two contracts at $5.00, I bought two more at $4.94. Then it went up to $5.12. Would most people sell out at $5.12? Not if the target was $7.00. So I would have held on, looking to buy more if it dropped. Going with this scenario, when silver began its decline, it's reasonable to assume that I would have bought more at $5.06 and again at $5.00, especially since that buy at $4.94 had encouraged me to buy the dip. Of course, when it hit $4.94, I would have bought a couple more (my lucky number, $4.94, hmmm?). And so, there I would have been, long my 10 contracts, with an average cost of $4.98. Once silver hit $4.92, I would have had a loss of six cents per ounce on 50,000 ounces, or $3,000. But, you say, that's the same loss.

You're right, but in the real world, it doesn't go that way. By training myself to buy the dips, I'm now in a mental state of mind that dictates holding on. After all, lower prices are a buying, not a selling, opportunity. And so, if silver were to decline to $4.50, the loss would balloon to $25,000 or so. Would a dip buyer set a protective stop? Perhaps, but I'll bet that if you have ever bought dips, you didn't have a protective stop on. Dip buyers don't.

The message is clear. If I was right and silver was going to $7.00, then it wouldn't make a large difference if my average cost were $5.00 or $5.10 or even $5.25. Even $5.25 would have yielded a profit of $87,500—still acceptable versus a $100,000 target. But, most important,

I would have been buying more as the market confirmed my opinion. It would have put me in a better frame of mind. If market movement increased my risk, at least that would have been within the context of price movement in my favor. And every time I bought more, the position I already held would have shown a larger and larger profit.

Finally, buying more as it moves in your favor also prevents you from loading up on losers. By definition, if you buy the dip, you're buying a loser.

Think of it this way: If, over 30 years of investing, you only back up the truck on your winners, don't you think you'll do better than if you're in the habit of shoveling in the losers?

AVOID
"THE BIG MISTAKE."

Every week I write an e-mail newsletter for our clients. And once in a while, I have a section called, "The Big Mistake."

The markets are ruthless. They seek out your weaknesses and play on them. Perhaps the most ruthless attribute of the markets is this: You can make 1,000 correct decisions. You can be right 1,000 times in a row. You can be perfect for 40 years and accumulate all kinds of wealth. But you only have to be very wrong once to completely undo being right 1,000 times.

This is obvious when you think about it, but most people don't. The problem lies in the fact that accumulation of wealth occurs in pieces but is destroyed en masse. Consider this:

You have come to the conclusion that you have figured out the mystery of the market. You and the market are one with the universe. You are a child of the market and it cannot and will not hurt you. And so, you "invest" all of your money in XYZ Widget Corporation. Lo and behold, the gods smile on you, and your $10,000 is turned into $20,000. Selling XYZ, you buy ABC Widgets (a downtrodden competitor) and poof! Right again: $20,000 turns into $30,000.

Amalgamated Mousetrap, Omnivore Corporation, Tweedle Dee Tweedle Dum Ltd., and Lotus Position Pharmaceuticals—one by one, you rattle off the winners, plowing your ever-increasing stake into each. Eventually, you've hit 25 out of 25.

Number 26 is an "on-fire" enterprise called St. John's Wort Amalgamated. It has discovered, you believe, a cure for anger. Unlimited possibilities! Unfortunately, after being right 25 times in a row, you're wrong on St. John's Wort, and the stock goes from $15 to $2 and then to zero. The Big Mistake.

The Big Mistake almost always involves taking on too much risk. It is the single large position whose decimating price move completely destroys the portfolio. The Big Mistake comes from hubris, ego, and greed. If, you reason, 10 percent of your portfolio invested in a single position is good, then 20 percent is better. And, if 20 percent, then why not 50?

To avoid The Big Mistake, you need to take tiny bites of each investment. This way, when you're wrong, you can survive.

You Pay a Premium
for Peace of Mind.

Human beings congregate in groups for safety and peace of mind. We tend to be tribal in our social behavior and this carries over into how we invest.

Most people are uncomfortable being alone. Most do not feel safe investing in downtrodden stocks that go unloved by most of the investing public. While we talk about being independent and acting on our own, in truth, most of us follow the crowd. We wait for some expert (opinion maker) to show us the way. This is why a stock will pop on a bullish article in *The Wall Street Journal* or after a favorable mention on financial television.

The result is that when you let others do your thinking—to give yourself the peace of mind that comes with grazing in a herd—you pay a price for that comfort. The price is put into the stock and the stock is marked up accordingly before you buy it.

The secret to making money is to get to these stocks before others do. That way, they're not marked up in price before you've had a chance to buy them. Buy before others do if you want to get the best price possible. This means that you'll have to act independently. You'll need to work hard and do some original research instead of having others spoon-feed it to you.

Despite what some people believe, successful investing is very hard work. It takes a lot of thinking, planning, and discipline. But hard work pays off. You have a choice. Let the other investor do the work and charge you for it through a higher stock price—or do the work yourself and pocket the difference.

THE GREATER THE RISK,
THE GREATER THE REWARD—
BUT ONLY IF YOU'RE RIGHT.

The markets can mean so many things to so many people that we often lose sight of what markets really are. Similar to the blind men trying to describe an elephant by touching various places on its skin, we can each be right but miss the larger picture.

At their very core, the markets are risk-transfer mechanisms. One investor who's interested in reducing her risk sells an investment to an investor who's willing to take on risk. The buyer of risk expects to be paid for her efforts and so expects a profit. It is the effort to find those investments that may carry less risk for a given profit that is the basic task of all market participants.

That the markets reward the taking of risk is a given. If risk takers were not rewarded, the game would be over. Absent compensation, no one would assume risk. Of course, when markets go bad, there is a surplus of risk avoiders and a shortage of risk takers. Therefore, prices must adjust to encourage the risk takers—they fall.

Each time you engage the markets, remind yourself that the markets are a forum for transferring risk among market players. You are either taking on risk or throwing it off with your investment activity. When you begin to think of the market in these terms, it forces you to focus on your risk taking. In the end, this is the most important thing for an investor to do.

Playing in an arena that holds risk transfer as its central theme, you had better pay attention to that central theme. Don't get sidetracked with earnings, chart resistance points, or interest rate divination. That's simply part of the effort to gauge whether you should be taking on or throwing off risk.

SELLING—

It's What's Left That Counts

DON'T BE A
STOCK COLLECTOR.

One of the more bizarre incidents that I've experienced in over 20 years of looking at portfolios was when a prospective client came into the office for an appointment. (You've probably been in a similar appointment. You bring your statements and you chat with the advisor as part of your shopping for a new one.) We'll call this client Joe.

After about 30 minutes of preliminaries, I asked to see his statements. There were over 150 investment positions (my eyes were probably the size of small plates) in a $1.2 million portfolio. This included well over 100 individual equities and probably three dozen mutual funds.

I am convinced to this day that Joe probably had every tax return he ever filed (all the way back to 1957) as well as every grocery store receipt, shoe box, and theater ticket stub that ever passed his way.

I advised him that no human being alive could get a handle on a portfolio like that without spending countless hours working on correlations and performance histories. No accountant who ever reared up on two legs would want to try to compute all the dividends, capital gains, capital losses, stock split adjustments, and capitalization changes. And no advisor, your author included, would want to be responsible for a portfolio such as that.

I advised Joe that he had diversified to the point of nondiversification. No doubt, a detailed and expensive study would show that his portfolio moved with the Wilshire 5000 stock index, minus fees.

Joe was a collector, not an investor. Unable to sell, unable to resist a daily dose of advice, he always bought a little of this, a little of that. If he got a tip over lunch, that was good for 50 or 100 shares. If *Forbes* ran a mutual funds article, he had to own a couple thousand each of two or three of the funds mentioned. On and on it went.

And so, who knew how he was doing? He didn't. Creator of the hundred-headed monster, fearful of what lurked in the basement of his financial net worth, he reached out, in furtive nervousness, for someone to put the sword to the monster.

My advice to Joe was quite simple. "Joe, we've got to take a meat cleaver to this. The capital gains aren't an issue, so taxes won't be a problem. If you're going to be a client, I want you to liquidate, probably, 80 percent of this stuff from a sell list we'll draw up for you and then you sell 'em where they are and bring us a check and we'll start fresh and focus your efforts."

As in "Casey at the Bat," I'm hopeful that somewhere the sun shines all the time, that all of Joe's investments have worked out just fine, and that he slew the dragon before it ate him. I wouldn't know. Joe's future was hidden from me by the cloud of dust raised by the beating of his feet out the door and into the parking lot. I ran after him. "Hey, you dropped some of your statements."

EXIT STRATEGY IS MORE IMPORTANT
THAN ENTRY STRATEGY.

Tune into any financial news program and you'll find that, as a matter of course, a guest is asked, "What are you buying now?" It's a reasonable question. People always like to know what other people—especially professionals—are buying.

But something is missing. If nearly 100 percent of the questions are about buying, half of the investing equation is being ignored. After all, when investing, you eventually sell what you buy; therefore, selling is half of your activity. And if half of your work involves selling, it should also command half of your time.

In my experience the overwhelming majority of investors are almost exclusively concerned with buying. They look constantly for new profit opportunities. They forget that in order to realize those profits, they have to be skilled in selling what they've bought. Given the lack of study given to proper selling technique, it's no wonder that most people tell you that knowing when to sell is hard.

Whenever you enter a position, remember that you'll only realize a profit if you have good closing technique. You need to be just as expert in exiting as in entering. It's like going into the theater. Don't you always take note of the EXIT sign? Even subconsciously? When you settle into your airline seat, the flight attendant points out the EXIT rows and doors. They want you to be able to get out of a burning theater or plane in an emergency.

Could you point out the EXIT rows in your portfolio?

SOMETIMES THE WHOLE
IS **NOT** EQUAL TO THE
SUM OF ITS PARTS.

In a reverse split, a large number of shares are called in and a fewer number are issued. For instance, a one-for-five split on a $2 stock with 1,000,000 shares outstanding should theoretically create 200,000 shares at $10 per share. The market capitalization of $2,000,000 stays the same. However, once a reverse split is completed, the market value of the company often falls.

Reverse splits are usually a sign of difficulty. Unable to get the stock price up through earnings improvements, the reverse split is used to soak up stock and raise the price. It's almost as though the reverse split focuses everyone's attention on the poor price of the stock and the—presumably—poor underlying fundamentals.

NEVER FORGET
UNCLE SAM.

It can't be said too often: Taxes are, far and away, the biggest drag on investment performance. Commissions pale by comparison. Investors fret endlessly about saving $5 or $10 on a trade, while the tax bill on that trade can amount to thousands—much of it probably unnecessary.

In order to work with my trading account, I have an Excel workbook on my laptop. The workbook contains 13 worksheets, each devoted to a different aspect of my strategy. Every stock position has a column showing the date of purchase and another column that automatically alerts me 30 days in advance of when that position is going to go long term, from a tax perspective.

You see, the short-term capital gains tax rate is about twice that of the long-term rate. A short-term $10,000 gain gets clipped by about $4,000 in taxes, while the same gain in long-term mode results in roughly a $2,000 tax. In short, by waiting a few days, I can often save 50 percent on my state and federal tax bills.

The converse is true when I have a loss: I'd much rather take that loss as a short-term than a long-term event. As a long-term event, I'd lose a big chunk of the tax savings I get from writing off the loss.

This is especially handy when I make multiple purchases of the same stock, which I often do when trading (when I invest, I tend to make a single purchase only). If I can avoid a short-term gain or avoid a loss going long-term, just two or three times each year, I offset all of my trading costs (commissions, exchange fees, etc.) with the tax reduction.

Taxes are my biggest investment expense, by far. And since I treat my investing like the business that it is, I pay close attention to my expenses. If I can reduce my expenses, I can increase my profits. After all, that's what the entire investing exercise is all about.

WHERE THERE'S
SMOKE, THERE'S FIRE.

Many times in recent years, I've seen firms (including some with wonderful corporate or brand names) disclose bookkeeping problems, sometimes within companies they acquired. But fraud disclosures, more often than not, are like cockroaches: If you see one, you know that there are others hiding in the woodwork. Often, the first disclosure of fraud is followed by other revelations that, at best, hold the stock price down and, at worst, send it lower.

Fraud often creates dead money until full discovery of the facts and management workout of the problems. Often, prices continue to decline due to all the uncertainty created by fraud. These disclosures are usually accompanied by analyst downgrades. Those downgrades are the opposite of a "catalyst" needed to move the stock higher. Sell the stock, cut your losses, and move on to better opportunities.

DON'T PRUNE YOUR FLOWERS AND
WATER YOUR WEEDS.

"Sell your losers and let your winners run." Sounds simple and logical, right? If you pare your losers, you'll eventually end up with a portfolio consisting mostly of winners. You'd think we'd all do it automatically, but, too often, investors do just the opposite. They hold their losers, hoping to recoup their losses, and sell their winners. What sense does that make?

Not much, but taking a loss is painful. As a result, we hold onto our losers, hoping against hope that their fortunes (and ours) will turn around. More often than not, that doesn't happen. Indeed, we watch as our stocks drop deeper into the red. At the same time, there's a real temptation to lock in profits on our winners, so we sell too soon and stand by as the price of the stock goes higher and higher.

The key to a flourishing portfolio is to let your winners blossom and to nip your losses in the bud. If you think about it, that makes intuitive sense. The object of investing is to make a profit. Losers rob you of capital, sometimes geometrically. Studies show that stocks that make new highs are apt to do so again, while stocks that hit new lows are at the very least unproductive for a while. Worse, they often are destined to hit lower lows.

SELL WHEN THE
STORY CHANGES.

When we buy stocks, we usually make the move for one or all of these reasons:

- Our analysis tells us the stock is undervalued compared to what we think the company will earn.

- Price or volume trends suggest the stock is moving higher.

- Developments involving the company or its industry sector promise to carry the stock higher.

In essence, when we consider buying a stock, we fashion a "story" that becomes the case for purchasing the shares. Say we're looking at the technology arena and focus on the mass-storage market, which boasts players such as IBM Corp., EMC Corp., and Storage Technologies. Our story might go something like this:

With the explosion of the Internet, all that data (the millions of website pages, for example) has to reside somewhere, which will heighten the demand for information storage. That's going to boost demand for mass-storage devices, which should make for some good action in these stocks.

Realizing it's sound investing to buy a few of these stocks instead of making one big bet, you purchase three of the industry leaders. Two behave as predicted and begin to trend higher soon after you buy them. A third stock is even more impressive, jumping five points (about 20 percent) in fairly short order. Indeed, it looks as if it's about to take off, and the analysts are boosting their ratings on the shares.

But when the story changes, it changes quickly. The stock drifts back a bit, which you attribute to consolidation after the strong run. But then your third company issues an earnings warning and the shares plunge, settling at a price just below what you paid originally. You should sell out.

When a stock's story changes, it usually means that its prospects are no longer consistent with your original investment thesis. What's more, the company has disappointed Wall Street (and its analyst sponsors), a crime in today's investment environment. It often means the stock's price is going nowhere, at least for a quarter or two, sometimes much longer. The point is, the story has changed for the worse, and that's reason to sell.

SELL WHEN THE STOCK EXCEEDS THE
PRICE TARGET YOU ESTABLISHED
WHEN YOU BOUGHT IT.

Successful investing is more than successful stock picking. This is particularly true of stocks bought for a quick trade. Clearly, we always have to make a sound case for buying a stock—there has to be a "story." But we also need to know what we plan to do with the stock once we own it. That means having a game plan.

As a cornerstone of that game plan or strategy, we should always have in mind a price target for each stock we buy. If we've crafted a sound rationale, making the case for buying a stock, we should have some idea of how we expect that stock to perform. And that means having set a price at which to sell.

Establishing a target doesn't necessarily mean that you have to sell the stock as soon as it hits that price. The company's story may have changed by then—earnings might exceed estimates, for instance—making it worthwhile to continue to hold the stock. However, if a stock hits the price target you set when you purchased, it's a signal that it's time to reevaluate.

Perhaps the stock is going no higher, in which case you should cut it loose and deploy the capital into a better investment. A money market account is a better investment than a stock that's going to tread water or go down.

On the other hand, especially in a powerful bull market, we often underestimate the force driving a stock higher. We're not just talking about a stock that is continuing to rise because the market is rising; that is because "new" buyers are climbing aboard only because the stock's price is rising. We're talking about having picked a winner, locking onto a stock that's massively undervalued, whose earnings are exploding and that's hitting repeated new highs. Such stocks, particularly those riding powerful secular trends, can often blow right through our conservatively calculated price targets. When that happens, sometimes you find yourself strapped on a rocket—enjoy the ride!

You don't want to cast aside your winners (cut your flowers) to keep your losers (water your weeds). When you've chosen well, hang on. Ratchet your price targets higher, but keep tabs on how well your investment is doing.

EASY COME,
EASY GO.

Sell when you reap an outsized gain in a very short period of time (for instance, 80 percent in a month). On occasion, an investment will move dramatically—20, 30, or 40 percent—in your favor in a very short period of time. This is usually caused by some news that has propelled the price of the position.

While it is true that news is often fully discounted over a longer period of time than that immediately following the news, it may still make sense to let a quick profit go quickly. A rapid move, especially in a stock, can often be caused by short sellers having to immediately buy back short positions. This is often a one-time phenomenon that is followed by a settling back of the stock. You can reestablish your position at a lower price or move on to something else.

AFTER A DIVIDEND IS CUT,
SHARES TEND TO LAG THE MARKET.

A cut in the dividend is always painful for a company. It is a public admission that the company must conserve its cash and that the upturn in the company's prospects is several quarters away. Otherwise, the dividend would not be cut.

When the dividend is cut, it doesn't necessarily mean that the stock is going lower. Sometimes, the cut is the coup de grace on a stock decline and the stock can stabilize after that happens. The market usually senses this in advance and discounts it before it happens.

But, it is also fair to say that the stock is usually dead money for some time to come and can be exited to free up capital for more productive purposes.

WHEN SENTIMENT BECOMES
TOO BULLISH, IT'S TIME TO SELL.

Euphoric price moves are tough to play. You want to lock in profits before they evaporate, but you don't want to get out too soon, since mini-manias can persist for months or even years. Market historians say speculative frenzies thrive on the so-called greater-fool theory—a belief that, no matter how foolishly high a price you pay, another fool will come along to take the stock off your hands at an even higher price.

It is notoriously difficult to judge these things, but here are a few signs to look for:

- Heavy insider selling in the stock after a big price run-up.

- Consistently positive news on the company that is widely disseminated.

- Difficulty imagining what could possibly drive the stock price lower.

- Basic valuation measures such as P/E ratios at the high end of the historic record for the stock.

- A 100 percent move in the stock, or more.

All of these factors point to the same thing. The story is widely known, investors have acted on it, the price reflects this bullishness, and insiders (those who know the company best) are selling into the rally.

Sometimes you sell one of these stocks and it keeps right on going. But you would be surprised how often a sale amid a rally can keep you out of trouble.

NOTHING'S PERFECT
ALL THE TIME.

Think of valuation measures like a violin string. The higher the values, the tighter the string. The lower the values, the looser the string. Now, if you pluck a tightly pulled string with ever increasing force, you're going to break the string, and when you do, it's going to snap and recoil with some real energy. Conversely, you can pluck away on a loosely wound string—it takes a lot more force to break it.

So it is with valuations. A stock sporting a triple-digit price/earnings ratio will sound sweet every time you pluck it . . . the stock moves higher. But as it does, you need more force (buying power) to drive it higher. At some point, it breaks and comes cascading down.

Stocks that are like this are often called "priced to perfection." All I can say about this is that the world is not a perfect place. If you own a stock priced to perfection, you'd better sell at the first sign of imperfection. As a matter of fact, you might sell a "perfect" stock as soon as someone pronounces it as such. "Early" is infinitely preferable to "late" in these things.

SOMETIMES,
YOU JUST GET LUCKY.

Have you ever entered into a position, and for some reason completely unrelated to your investment thesis, the position moved to a big profit? If that happens, sell and get out. You were lucky. And when you're lucky, admit it and take your profit.

I can remember purchasing a block of Aetna for our clients' contrarian accounts. I had worked on an analysis of AET after watching the stock plunge over 50 percent. Earnings worries created by a tough pricing environment, combined with an earnings warning from the company and the subsequent earnings shortfall, cratered the stock. I thought I saw good value and bought the stock, with a goal of a 50 percent gain. Completely out of the blue, a tender offer was made for the company. While it was eventually rebuffed, I didn't wait around. I sold.

I could have reasoned that the acquirer saw the same value I did. I could have argued with myself that my thesis still held and that I should stick around. However, a possible takeover of the company was never in my mind. But once that surfaced, some of the undervaluation was taken out, and I was then operating in an environment best left to arbitrageurs.

Although we didn't get our 50 percent profit, I knew we had been lucky. As I said, the buyout was eventually rejected, but even had it gone through at a still higher price, I wouldn't have looked back. Lucky is lucky, and I can't count on luck. Neither should you.

SPECULATION—
Throwing the Dice

DON'T TRY TO
CATCH A FALLING KNIFE.

When a stock, commodity, or option goes into free-fall, there are always those who buy into that decline. It's a bad idea.

First, by buying into a free-fall decline, you are buying into a position in which obviously some news is moving the market. Whether you believe the news or not, the rush of the moment doesn't allow for thoughtful analysis, so you must begin by assuming that the market is right and that the news is meaningful. That would tell you to wait.

Second, buying into a free-fall means that you're investing against the trend, and as we all know, the trend is your friend. You need very strong reasons to bet against a trend—your gut instinct isn't enough. So a free-fall purchase is, in reality, a countertrend trade, which is always an iffy proposition.

Third, by buying into a free-fall, you are actually trying to pick off the bottom—a nearly impossible task. If you ever actually succeed in doing so, it is usually more a matter of luck than skill. If you try picking the bottom a dozen times, you're actually going to do it once or twice.

Let's face it. People buy into declines because the price looks cheap. But the new "cheap" price is quite probably the new high price. Something has changed. Recognize that change, have patience, and let it all settle down before you take a serious look.

NEVER BUY
ON MARGIN.

Another word for margin is *leverage*. When you margin a position, you borrow money using your position as collateral, investing the new funds in additional positions. A little math makes it clear:

You own 1,000 shares of XYZ at $20 per share. Convinced it is going higher, you borrow an additional $10,000, using your stock as collateral, and buy more. You now own 1,500 shares and you owe your broker $10,000. A surprise shortfall in earnings drives the stock down to $12 overnight. Your 1,500 shares are now worth only $18,000. But you still owe your broker $10,000. Your net after-loan position has gone from a value of $20,000 to $8,000. Had you not margined the position, you would own $12,000 worth of XYZ.

Margin magnifies moves, both up and down. But, perhaps more important, margin magnifies your emotions. It supercharges what you feel, both good and bad. When the position is moving against you, your fears are magnified, and when it is moving in your favor, it fuels your greed.

This means that your mind is clouded just when clear thinking is at a premium. Thus, the first victim of a margined position is clear thinking.

Margin also tends to play havoc with your risk control. While $20,000 represented 10 percent of a $200,000 portfolio, the new $30,000 position is 15 percent of your portfolio—a 50 percent increase in the risk of the position. Presumably, when you paid cash for the first portion of the position, you computed your risk and felt that 10 percent was a reasonable amount. In your excitement (destabilized mental condition), you threw that risk control out the window and leveraged the position.

Last, but definitely not least, margin can be like a drug. The worst thing that can happen to you is to score the first time you use margin. No, maybe that's not the worst thing that can happen. What is worse still is that you win the second time. Now, utterly convinced that you can accelerate your travel down the road to riches, you pile it on the third time.

That's probably when Mr. Market calls a halt to your foolishness.

"ANTHONY, SOMETIMES THEY JUST
WANT TO BUY 'EM."

A broker and friend said this to me back in the early 80s. He was a guy who remembered posting quotes on a blackboard with chalk. He's passed on now, but I've always remembered his words.

He made this comment in answer to my wonderment that people were pushing the price of oil and gas stocks higher and higher. Unless you really believed the forecasts of $100-per-barrel oil, the prices of the stocks were way, way out of line with fundamentals.

His point was that when people want to own something, they will create whatever justification they need in order to make the trade. Back in the early 80s oil was going to $100 and gold was $1,000 an ounce. In 1999, earnings didn't matter and P/Es were irrelevant. In both cases, people just wanted to buy 'em, so reason gave way to emotion.

This is an obvious but important point to remember. People will give you all kinds of theory and reasons why you should pay 400 times earnings for a stock. It will sound perfectly rational. More often that not, it's "them" just wanting to buy 'em.

STOCKS—

A Piece of the Future

IF YOU WANT A FRIEND,
GET A DOG.

Don't kid yourself. That hot little stock that just rocketed up 50 percent yesterday is not your friend. It is not your buddy. And, because it isn't your friend or your spouse, you should not fall in love with it.

It can be vicious. It can turn on a dime and sink its teeth into you. Whatever you do, don't fall in love with an investment. You want friendship? Get a dog. You want trouble? Fall in love with your investments.

DON'T PUT ALL YOUR EGGS
IN ONE BASKET.

This is one of the most difficult issues any investor can face.

Many companies reward employees with stock options, stock grants, or the ability to purchase stock at a discount from market value. So the stock granted is a bargain. It makes good sense to take advantage of your employer's program. The question is, how much of your portfolio should be held in your company's stock?

I've wrestled with this question for 20 years, both for myself and on behalf of many clients from many companies.

From a strict risk-control perspective, you shouldn't have more than 10 to 15 percent of your portfolio in your employer's stock. Assuming your company is an industry leader, you can consider that stock a proxy for its industry. I don't like to put more than 15 percent of a portfolio in any single industry, but recognizing that this is impossible when you have unvested stock options or restricted stock positions, we need to broaden the guideline and see how we can work with it.

Another rule of thumb, with which I agree, is not to tie up more than 50 percent of your net worth in your employer's stock. On the downside, this means that if the stock drops by half, your net worth drops by one-quarter (one-half of one-half). While this certainly is a wrenching blow, it is generally not a financially crippling one. Conversely, if the position grows to exceed 50 percent, I recommend that you pare some back or reduce your purchases to slow the growth.

Your other investments need to take into account the outsized risk your employer's stock represents. Consider employees at Xerox Corporation in 2000. They watched their company stock plummet from $65 to $15 in a matter of months. Imagine spending 25 years working for a company, accumulating stock until you owned 25,000 shares. Then, only weeks before retirement, you watch the value fall from $1,625,000 to $375,000. Decades of patient accumulation undone in a matter of months. (This, of course, is the risk in any individual stock.)

Here's my advice: If you work for a computer manufacturer, for example, and are part of a stock plan, don't invest *any* other money in high technology. By owning your employer's stock, you already own a lot of high technology. Limit your other investments to areas that don't correlate highly with high technology—REITs for instance.

When doing your asset allocation, don't forget to include all of the stock you own. Whether restricted stock, unvested options (use the spread between the option cost and the current market price as your value), or stock owned outright, include all of it in your asset allocation as large cap, small cap, or whatever appropriate asset class it represents.

Don't become obsessed with accumulating shares. Sometimes people just like to count the number they own, and as that number grows, they become increasingly obsessed with making it grow larger. That can be an empty exercise.

If the stock has an outsized move, a particularly big year that defied all of your expectations, then consider selling some off and paying down your mortgage. If possible, pay off the entire mortgage. Remember, until you've sold some stock, you haven't made anything on it. You have no profit. Everything is on paper until you sell. By taking the concrete step of paying off a mortgage, you're transferring assets into a measurable improvement in your life. No matter what may come your way, you own your own home.

When a company gets into trouble, downsizing is common. The worst thing that can happen is to not only watch the stock tumble, but to get caught in the downsizing and lose your job as well. The history of the markets is replete with investors who stayed too long, who were welcomed to a party, but just didn't know when to go home.

Just remember this: You are not betraying your employer by securing your family's future. You are not showing a lack of gratitude by protecting your family. Employers give stock benefits to their employees as compensation for a job well done. It isn't actually compensation until you cash it in.

STOCKS FALL FASTER
THAN THEY RISE.

One of the difficulties of investing in the market is that you can work very hard, for a long time, to get your way up, only to see the market crash down in a fraction of the time. Stocks and markets fall faster than they rise.

I've often thought about why this is true. After all, you would expect things to rise as quickly, or as slowly, as they fall. What is it about a drop that results in a faster pace?

I think it goes something like this: When a company's business is going well, it's an incremental thing—perhaps a new product this quarter, better sales forecast for next year, some unexpected cost reductions. All of this good news is announced as it happens, because any good news is good news to bring public. As a result, you get a constant drip of public relations announcements and corporate feel-good pronouncements. As each small piece of good news is announced, it's reflected in the stock price, which moves irregularly higher.

Bad news, which drives stocks down, is different. When a company has a small piece of bad news, there is a natural tendency either to not announce it or to hold it back and work on the problem. Since these small pieces of bad news aren't market moving, the company really isn't violating its public trust. You know, such and such a production line went down for two hours last night, but at some point, enough production lines go down enough times to warrant an announcement: "We're having major league problems with our production and it's affected our ability to deliver orders." Boom! Down goes the stock. Put another way, it seems that the bad news is accumulated and then released when it's so big that a release is required. Good news is good news and released at any time.

I also believe stocks drop faster than they rise because of the "absence of buyers" phenomenon. When a stock is rising, there is generally a good supply of both buyers and sellers. When bad news hits, most people (buyers and sellers alike) freeze, so it is the marginal buy or sell that affects the stock price. Volume dries up, leaving only motivated sellers, who drive the market down. Given the absence of buyers, stocks are marked down quickly and by a lot.

THERE IS NO FREE LUNCH
IN THE MARKETS.

Stocks with superhigh yields may be poised for a dividend cut. This rule is one to consider for bonds too, although there is a place for high-yielding bonds (so-called junk bonds) in an investor's portfolio.

There is no free lunch in the markets. They're too deep and too efficient for you to find glaring opportunity. So when you look at two utility stocks, and one yields 6 percent while the other offers 12 percent, you can bet that the lower-yielding stock is in much better financial condition, with a history of dividend increases on a fairly regular basis. The 12 percent stock probably hasn't had a dividend increase in years, finances may be weak, and a dividend cut may be in the cards.

If you have two similar stocks (two REITs or two utilities), the lower-yielding one is usually the better investment.

LOOK FOR THE
SILVER LINING.

When the Fed tightens interest rates, the yield curve will often invert. This simply means that short-term interest rates are than longer-term interest rates. As this happens, utilities and other interest-sensitive stocks (bank stocks, for example) fall off in price as the cost of money rises.

But, even as these equity prices fall, it is a point of interest to the prudent speculator that an inverted yield curve is not a normal one, and depressed prices beckon examination for capital commitment.

I have generally found that an inverted yield curve offers an opportunity to buy utility and other interest-sensitive stocks at a discount. Inverted curves aren't the norm and should be exploited for opportunity.

THERE'S GOLD IN THEM
THAR HILLS, BUT GETTING
IT AIN'T ALWAYS EASY.

Buying gold is not as risky as buying gold stocks, but the stocks are the preferred investment. When you buy a gold mining stock, you get the effect of leverage, so your investment dollar goes further. While buying a gold mining stock might seem, at first glance, to be less risky than buying the metal, a little math will convince you otherwise.

Let's say Sam's Mine produces gold for $200 an ounce. If the current gold price is $300 per ounce, Sam's Mine can make $100 per ounce of gold. If there are 1,000,000 shares of Sam's Mine outstanding, and they produce 5,000 ounces of gold, Sam's profit is $500,000 (50 cents per share).

Now, look what happens if the price of gold moves up 10 percent to $330 per ounce. Sam's profits per ounce rise from $100 to $130—an increase of 30 percent. Profits per share are now 65 cents, also an increase of 30 percent. If the P/E ratio remains the same, Sam's Mines common moves up 30 percent in price.

You can see how a 10 percent increase in the price of gold resulted, in this case, in a 30 percent increase in the stock price. Roughly, then, in the case of Sam's Mine, it takes only about one-third the investment in the stock to equate to the same upside potential as the metal. Of course, the effect cuts both ways—any decrease in the price of gold hits profits pretty hard.

Generally, in a bull market for gold, you want to own the stocks. And in a bear market, you want to own the metal because the leverage to the downside is absent, but you still have exposure. And in a real rip-roaring bull move, junior mining stocks have the most leverage of all.

You don't have to make the stock selection complicated. Pick two or three big gold mining stocks. You can pick them by market cap, by profits, or whatever. They all tend to move together.

One caveat: Do a little homework and see how much forward selling, or hedging, has been done. If they've already sold their production forward at fixed prices, leverage is muted.

AVOID "TSELs"
IN FAVOR OF "GARPs."

The stocks everybody loves (TSELs) are highly risky because they've typically been bid up to fully priced levels, while the growth-at-a-reasonable-price stocks (GARPs) tend to be trading at P/E levels that are less than their growth rates—making them potential bargains.

As a rule, you want to be buying stocks when their P/E ratio is less than the growth rate of earnings. So if earnings are growing at 30 percent per year, you'd like the stock sporting a P/E ratio of less than 30. However, you sometimes need to adjust this. It is, for instance, difficult to buy a technology bellwether at a PEG ratio of less than 1.0.

The PEG ratio (aka GARP) helps relate growth to the price you pay for that growth—a useful barometer for stock selection.

Style—

It's a Matter of Taste (and Comfort)

THERE ARE NO
EASY ANSWERS.

A couple of years ago, I debated a well-known market guru who was known for his strong views on indexing. Our audience was a group of financial planners and advisors, and since they overwhelmingly use actively managed funds and managers, it's not surprising that I got the most votes in the debate.

Is indexing better than active investing? The answer is, it depends.

It's been my experience that in deep and liquid markets—such as for U.S. Treasuries, or large-cap U.S. stocks—it is very difficult to consistently beat a broad index. If you assume that 1,000 market participants collectively have more wisdom than one, then you can see how the odds begin to tilt away from you.

But this doesn't give indexing a free ride. In markets where information isn't as readily available or participation isn't as deep, I do believe indexing can be a subpar strategy. I've just seen too many examples of small-cap and international managers who have consistently beaten their market indexes for me to believe that it can't be done.

I'm not sure that I believe that a Warren Buffett proves the case against indexing. I think it is reasonable to assume that the qualities needed to beat the markets are so difficult to gather that a Buffett can be considered to be an aberration of a very large statistical population. I have often wondered who Buffett's opposite is? Somewhere, there must exist the anti-Buffett who consistently underperforms the market in the same spectacular way.

To tell the truth, I use both indexing and active investing in my portfolios. I think indexing has a place. But I am equally convinced that a pure indexing approach is not a practical solution for most investors.

Actually, I don't get too hung up on the whole thing. In the end, if you get reasonably good returns, whether or not they trail an index, you tend to be generally satisfied with what you achieved.

IF THE SHOE FITS,
BUY IT.

You can use both active and passive management in your portfolio. There is an endless debate among investors as to whether active portfolio management or indexing (passive investing) is the best way to go. In listening to the debate, you can feel that you've got to make your call and jump into one camp or the other because one is right and one is wrong. I couldn't disagree more.

First, there is compelling evidence that in the most efficient markets, such as large-capitalization U.S. stocks, passive investment is a viable strategy. Most investors have a great deal of difficulty beating a big index such as the S&P 500 or the Dow Jones Industrial Average. On the other hand, the evidence is also strong that in less efficient markets, such as international and small cap, many practitioners can beat the index.

What's an investor to do?

I think your response can be one, or the other, or both. If transaction costs and management fees drive you nuts, then by all means gather a bunch of indexes together, allocate your capital, and go to the golf course, or go shopping, or lay on the beach. Reallocate two to four times per year and that's that.

On the other hand, if the thought of your net worth tied up in autopilot strategies makes you nervous, perhaps indexing isn't for you. In that case, hire managers, or buy funds, or manage some or all of it yourself.

For those of us not seeking a religious experience, both can make sense. For instance, in my 401(k), where we have mutual funds available, I use two active funds and one index fund. I'm perfectly content with that.

Some investors will buy a big index, such as the S&P 500 or Wilshire, through exchange-traded funds or index mutual funds as their core portfolio. Then they use active management for the less accessible markets—small cap, emerging, and international markets. Or they do it the other way around—index the small stuff and go active on big-cap American stocks.

In the end, do what suits your personality. If you miss a few points of performance, but you're happier than you would be chasing the last dollar, then be happy. Indexing can bring out the zealots like nothing else. Indexing is their thing in life and it's fine for them. It doesn't have to be yours or mine, so feel free to walk around where you wish.

MATCH YOUR PLAN
TO YOUR RESOURCES.

In developing an investment style, you need to begin with an honest appraisal of your resources and what return you can realistically hope to achieve.

People tend to think about how much money they want to make, and then begin to invest to reach that goal. You may decide that you want to make $100,000 in the market. Fine. That's a good goal. However, if you only have $10,000 to invest, you would have to double your money $3\frac{1}{4}$ times in order to reach that goal. Put another way, if you give yourself three years to reach your target, you need an annual return of something around 120 percent per year. A target such as that forces you into wildly speculative plays all of the time. The odds, by definition, are heavily against you. The likely result is that you'll find yourself, at some point, with large losses, leaving you further than ever from your goal.

If, on the other hand, you have $1,000,000 to invest, and you give yourself two years to make that same $100,000, you can throw the money in a money market fund and simply let the days tick off. Same goal, much different risk profile, and much greater chance of success.

In addition to considering the amount of capital you have, you need to consider the amount of time you can devote to managing your portfolio. The riskier the strategy, the more time you must devote to it to reach success. There is a direct correlation between the amount of risk involved and the time needed to work the portfolio.

Don't try to accomplish something beyond your grasp. Start slowly, take small risks, have modest expectations. Learn as you go, and invest with your eye firmly on long-term targets and goals. Too many investors are in a hurry. There is nothing in the stars that says that the markets are going to accommodate your needs. Your wanting to make 100 percent doesn't mean that the world will bend to your needs.

BE REALISTIC ABOUT WHAT
YOU CAN ACHIEVE.

Most investors set profit objectives—either a specific dollar amount or a percentage return they would like to achieve. In my experience, these profit objectives are often set without reference to what is achievable. Investors don't always distinguish between wishful thinking and achievable results.

Consider a man with $100,000 to invest. Now, a reasonable objective would be 9 percent per year ($9,000). The history of the markets indicates that a mix of about 80 percent stocks and 20 percent bonds should achieve that return over time. The objective is realistic in its goal and achievable with a reasonable investment policy. If the 80/20 asset allocation is followed, and the stock and bond selections are reasonable ones, then the probability of success is high.

Another investor wants to earn 12 percent per year. Again, this goal is a reasonable one, but the investor needs to know that only a fully invested equity portfolio will do the trick. This means that from time to time, a 20 percent loss is certainly probable and must be dealt with. Therefore, while the objective is reasonable and supported by historic return, its probability of success is a bit lower because the possibility is fairly strong that the investor could bail out in a bad market and not see the strategy through to the end.

The speculator might wish for a 20 percent annual return. This goal is difficult to achieve and requires not only a high degree of skill but also the willingness to assume leverage or investment in assets with a very high risk profile—emerging growth stocks, commodities, currencies, and so on. The probability of success is poor and the odds of significant draw down of capital are high.

When setting objectives, you need to take into account not only what is possible given the historic returns of the assets you intend to purchase but also your own personal weaknesses and tendencies.

Over time, most people are capable of sticking to a strategy that will produce an annual return of between 7 and 10 percent. Achieving higher returns becomes increasingly difficult because the risk profile of the investments needed brings into play the weaknesses and fears of most investors. A realistic objective has a high probability of success and so can often be achieved.

IF YOU DON'T UNDERSTAND IT, DON'T BUY IT.

In my opinion, the most compelling investment ideas are those explained in plain English. Consider the power of a plainly written sentence by Winston Churchill: "The most useful work of government is to put milk into babies." You can see the power of writing clearly.

When you've got the force of a compelling idea, simple words and clear argument convey it best. When the argument isn't on your side, then you finesse to make a point while hiding the truth. Consider these two brief investment opinions that I read in *Barron's* one Saturday afternoon:

"On the basis of enterprise value to calendar estimated gross profit, ABC Widgets currently trades at a multiple of eight times versus a comparable mean of 27 times. We feel the shares are currently undervalued. However, we have a cautious view on the company's ability to capture its revenue opportunity and await announcements of enterprise deployment and large customer wins to track the company's prospects going forward."

Now I have an MBA and I can tell you that I don't have a clue as to what is being said. Who teaches people to write like this? Compare that cloud within an enigma to the following, from another analyst, whose comments were adjacent to the other one's:

"We are lowering our earnings per share estimates to 94 cents and $1.21, respectively. We are also lowering our 12-month price target to $14 from $23."

Which analysis provides useful information?

You see, what happens is that some people fill the room with pixie dust. They use insider jargon in a clever way. To those in the know, they are making perfect sense—pixie dusters only make sense to other pixie dusters. As for readers who don't understand, such writers intimidate through their language. You'd feel stupid raising your hand and asking what "enterprise deployment" is. Never mind that no one else in the room understands it—they would never admit it. Frankly, I don't know what enterprise deployment is (I think it means executing your business plan and putting assets to work), but I can make an educated guess. Maybe we should attempt a rewrite:

"ABC Widgets has no earnings, so the value of the company is a guess. We think it's got a lot of potential, but we're concerned about sales. We'd like to see them close a couple of big contracts, which would give us some confidence in our ability to analyze their prospects. For now, it looks like a crap shoot, but at least it's an interesting crap shoot."

That, I can deal with!

Don't ever be intimidated. If after reading or listening, you still don't understand, pass. Worse, if you smell pixie dust, run away. If you see a gray fog rolling out from the podium, leave.

STICK TO
THE PROGRAM.

Momentum players look for companies whose stock price is on the move because of either steadily increasing earnings or rising investor interest in the sector. For momentum players, rising price is sometimes the only criterion for buying a stock. Cynics say this is little more than the greater-fool theory in action. At times, it seems a bit like casino capitalism.

Yet, momentum investing does have its rationale. Look to physics to understand just why. Newton's law tells us that an object in motion tends to stay in motion until acted upon by an opposing force. As it applies to stocks, it means stocks that are in motion and moving higher will keep moving in that direction until an opposing force stops them.

Studies have shown that stocks that hit new highs have a tendency to do so again. So red-hot shares may remain red-hot until an opposing force counters that rise. That new force could be new information such as slumping earnings, interest in a new sector, or a major reversal in the overall market.

Momentum players playing the earnings game are betting that earnings will continue to accelerate. That's the reason the stock is rising. Typically, those stocks trade at a big multiple to their rate of earnings growth. That puts them in risky territory, vulnerable to any changes in earnings growth or investor sentiment. If you're using the earnings-momentum strategy and earnings falter, it's best to punch out and parachute into a better-looking opportunity.

PEG THE PEG.

The PEG ratio is a great way to evaluate just how much you are paying for a company's earnings growth. The ratio is computed by dividing the price/earnings ratio by the earnings growth rate.

Example: A company sports a P/E ratio of 22. Earnings are growing at 32 percent per year: 22 divided by 32 yields a PEG ratio of 0.68.

Value investors look for stocks with PEG ratios of 1.0 or less. In other words, you want to pay less in terms of the P/E ratio than the rate of earnings growth. If the P/E is less than the growth rate, you are essentially getting earnings growth at a bargain price.

The PEG ratio is a great way to compare stocks of different growth rates on the same scale. This allows you to make an apples-to-apples comparison of two stocks whose growth rates might be wildly different:

ABC Utilities: P/E of 8, earnings growth rate of 5 percent per year

XYZ Widgets: P/E of 35, earnings growth rate of 25 percent per year

PEG of ABC: 8 ÷ 5 = 1.6

PEG of XYZ: 35 ÷ 25 = 1.4

So, just on an evaluation of how much you are paying for earnings, XYZ is the cheaper stock, even though it may, at first glance, appear to be the more expensive one.

I always check the PEG ratio on a stock I'm considering. And when I've got a choice between two stocks in the same industry and business, the PEG ratio can often break the tie.

TIMING–

It's All in It (or Is It?)

INVEST FOR
THE LONG RUN.

Whatever methodology or strategy currently has your interest, remember that you should never veer from the idea of investing for the long run.

Study after study has shown conclusively that it's time in the market, not market timing, that leads to great fortunes. You must have a core portfolio of key holdings that changes very little over time. These are the horses hitched to your financial wagon that will bring you home. They may be a group of mutual funds, a list of 20 stocks, or a mix of funds, stocks, and commodities.

Whatever your list, whatever your core portfolio, stay with it. In times of prolonged market declines, you may question why you are doing it. When the market is running and your group is lagging, you'll tend to mix it up, trying to fine-tune your performance. There are hundreds of distractions to cause you to abandon the idea of a core portfolio.

And, of course, the worst distraction is trading—especially after you've had a big profit. You begin to multiply the numbers. "If I only had all of my money trading, then my returns would be 52 percent per year, not just an additional 4 percent overall return. Maybe I should sell half of those stocks and put the capital into my system."

When you're tempted to do this, just remember that if you stick to good quality, diversify by industry and business, and buy industry leaders, it's a reasonably good formula for a good core portfolio. If you have a good core portfolio, you will capture the major returns offered by large-capitalization stocks over a long period of time. History says that's about 11 to 13 percent per year.

If you really don't feel comfortable picking those stocks, and you don't want an advisor, then buy three or four large diversified stock funds with a consistent performance history, or simply index that portion of your life and concentrate on your trading.

Set aside a portion of your capital for trading, where a speculative success with a small amount of capital can enhance return. That is, think of your core portfolio as an aircraft carrier surrounded by smaller ships. Protect that ship, but allow rapid movement around it. What you want to avoid is getting rid of the aircraft carrier.

Following this strategy allows for a lot of good things to happen. One of the best is to give you a win-win:

- If your trading is a disaster, you've preserved the bulk of your investment capital.

- If your trading is a success, you've enhanced your overall return.

Your core portfolio will almost certainly win for you if you diversify, pick good-quality stocks and/or funds, and maintain the portfolio for the long haul. Your trading is much more problematic and may or may not work for you. But, no matter. You've taken the right steps to avoid disaster.

It's time in the market, NOT market timing.

Don't time the market. Do I contradict myself? Not at all. You can be a stock picker, looking for individual opportunities to exploit, without being a market timer. Market timing involves moving your entire portfolio in and out of the market, trying to pick the exact low at which to buy and the exact high at which to sell. But it doesn't work. Sorry.

THE RULE OF THREE.

In *Pit Bull*, legendary S&P trader Marty Schwartz talks about his rule of three. The rule of three helps us understand how long it takes for news to be fully priced into a security. Generally, Schwartz suggests, by the third day, the news is in the price.

On the first day, the professionals, friends (and foes), daily market observers, and traders learn about the news and react by buying or selling. By the second day, clients of various brokers have all called them back and have acted. In addition, the analysts have had a chance to post their comments and their institutional clients have acted. By the third day, only a few people are coming into the market on the news, which means that, after a strong or weak opening, the stock will tend to settle down.

I like this rule. For one thing, it keeps me from acting too quickly on a new position. If I wait for the third day, I have to exercise patience so I won't make an emotional decision. This reduces my trading errors. It also gives me a time frame in which I can plan a trade (if any) and reminds me when I can see some settling down of the stock. That is another way of saying that the rule of three keeps me out until the market has expressed its opinion.

Now, I know that by doing that, I'm going to miss a profitable trade if I have some insight that tells me that the market has over- or underreacted to the news. I remember a front-page article in *The Wall Street Journal* about a major dot.com and the slowing of business resulting from doubts about the effectiveness of dot.com advertising. When I read the piece, I was short call options on the stock, looking for a decline or a treading of water. I thought the article, coming on top of a downgrade by a Lehman analyst, had to be a blow to the bulls. The stock opened down only $3 to $118 or so.

Now, every instinct was telling me to sell short more calls, that the market was going to price it a lot lower. But I didn't do the trade. Perhaps the only mildly weak opening indicated that the news was already in the stock, and I was just slow on the uptake. I should have traded—the stock closed down $8 on the day—but I don't regret not doing so.

I'm willing to pay that price because I know that, on average, the market is smarter than I am, so I am best served staying out until volatility has decreased and the market has spoken. Besides, in this case, I was already short, so I'd still profit if right.

DON'T MISTAKE
AGILITY FOR SUCCESS.

Even a gazelle must avoid a pride of lions. The market can be a brute, a beast. The fact that you're quick doesn't mean that you'll meet with success.

People take the ability to move in and out of the market for granted. They base trading systems and investment strategies on the belief that they can get in and out whenever they wish. They know that pricing might move against them, but they don't question liquidity. This mistake is made all the more dangerous by the fact that a single loss of liquidity can cause a fatal blow.

Many people today trade online. They enjoy zipping in and out of positions, taking pride in the fact that they may be in a position for only a matter of seconds or minutes. Let's examine that for a moment.

If they only hold a position for a very short period of time, then it stands to reason that most of the time they are attempting to scalp a small per-unit profit, perhaps ¼ or ½, on a stock. If you are going to make real money doing that (and it is, in my opinion, an awfully tough way to make money), then you need to lever up the position in order to make it worth your while. After all, if you make 25 cents per share, the profit on 100 shares gets eaten up in the commission and taxes.

So they lever up to 1,000, 2,000, or 5,000 shares. It is a bigger position than they should take on, but they do so *assuming that they can get out quickly.* Nearly every time, they can.

Now, even assuming that they never freeze at the switch (not a good assumption), all it takes is one stock halted for news to decimate a portfolio. A speculator buys 2,000 shares of a $50 stock (a $100,000 position) in a $200,000 account, looking to scalp a point on a bullish Tuesday morning. Suddenly, the stock is halted for news and the trap is sprung. A surprise earnings shortfall tanks the stock $15.

Taking liquidity for granted is a poor way to conduct an investment campaign. You always have to assume that just when you most need to get in or get out, you won't be able to. If you remember this, then you will begin to build in safeguards and think more in terms of survival than merely in terms of all-out, aggressive movement.

TRENDS—
What Goes Up Must Come Down (and Vice Versa)

THE TREND
IS YOUR FRIEND.

Good investments often work right from the very start. If I put on a position and that position is profitable from the day I enter it, it tends to work wonderfully well. I used to wonder about this. I'd wonder if I was cherry picking some anecdotal experience to fit a false view of the world, or if my success really was true.

Eventually, I concluded that this phenomenon is based on sound theory: If you put on a position and it moves in your favor, you've put on a position in the direction of the trend. If you sell soybeans short and they immediately fall five cents, the trend is moving your way. Also, your judgment is quickly being vindicated, which raises your confidence level. That, in turn, can help you to trade more profitably. It's much easier to trade with profits under your belt than with losses.

For me, an immediate profit is like a ladybug, a hummingbird, or a rainbow. It's good luck, good fortune, and wondrous beauty all at the same time.

Still, you shouldn't underestimate the difficulty of trading with the trend. If you want to buy at the bottom and sell at the top, it is almost impossible to do so if you trade with the trend. After all, at the top or bottom a trend has been in place and you're stepping right into it. When you trade with the trend, you need to carefully examine the investment for intrinsic value. If you're going long, you must be convinced that it has not yet reached full value. If you're going short, you must be convinced that it has not yet reached a bottom.

NOT ALL TRENDS
ARE EQUAL.

Everyone seems to agree that the trend is your friend, but if you ask people how they define a trend, you rarely get a coherent answer. It should be a simple thing, but it isn't.

The first problem you have in defining a trend is the time frame to use. You can look at a 30-day daily price chart and see a clear uptrend. But if you pan out to a 52-week chart, the same stock can exhibit a clear downtrend. And if you look at a five-year chart of monthly prices, you may find no trend at all. The same security can have three different trend characteristics.

The second problem is simply defining the trend. Trends are usually defined in terms of "higher highs and higher lows" for an uptrend or "lower highs and lower lows" for a downtrend. Unfortunately, it usually isn't that clear. You can have a series of higher highs and then suddenly a lower low, which reverses back to an uptrend.

Others will suggest drawing some kind of trend line connecting recent lows (for an uptrend) or recent highs (for a downtrend). All is well until a price spike violates the trend line and you're left wondering if the trend is intact or not.

Finally, it seems that once you're able to clearly identify a trend, it must be, by definition, well advanced. You are then faced with the problem that the trend has a stronger likelihood of reversing as it ages.

It's a devilish problem but one that must be solved if you are to be successful.

The answer is that there is no single answer. There is no single rule or group of rules that will take care of this problem for you. There are, however, some general guidelines that work:

1. Define the trend in terms of your trading time frame. If you are a long-term investor, then a trend should be defined with monthly or quarterly price charts. If you are a day trader, then your trend is defined with 5- or 10-minute charts.

2. Define the trend in context. If you are in a bull market and you're trying to decide if IBM is in an uptrend or not, the odds are that it is because the market is.

3. A trend should be obvious. If you find yourself peering at the chart and squinting your eyes, you are probably in a trading range and not in a trend.

4. If you draw a trend line and it is violated, redraw it assuming the trend is intact. If the new trend line is violated as well, you're probably heading into a trading range.

5. Trading ranges are the usual course of things, so give them the benefit of the doubt.

6. If you don't have higher highs and higher lows, you are not in an uptrend and vice versa. A quick glance at the chart should easily establish that for you.

7. Finally, you should generally find confirmation in other like securities that should make it easier for you. If you think gold is in an uptrend, silver should confirm that. If you think semiconductors are in a downtrend, another high-tech index or two should confirm it.

For every trend that I'm able to clearly identify and trade, I find 10 others that are suspect or unclear or that I consider unstable enough not to trade on. Finding trends can be a difficult and frustrating exercise, but it is one we must do.

GET A
WEATHER REPORT.

It is certainly more important to know the weather when you're trading commodities than when you're trading equities. You can't get involved in orange juice or grains or heating oil without an eye on the sky.

But every investor should have some macro-idea about the weather floating around in her strategy. It doesn't have to be complicated. It can be as simple as "This winter will be normal," or "This summer will be wet."

You can get these forecasts from the government, you can read and hear about them on the Weather Channel.

The weather can have such a huge impact on our markets and the economy that you just can't afford to ignore it. Most investors do. Most assume that they can't forecast it anyway. And, therefore, they underestimate its impact.

If it's going to be a cold winter, then heating costs will rise, which, in turn, is generally good for oil, natural gas, and other energy stocks. That, of course, can slow retail sales as people divert money to utilities instead of buying goodies at the mall. As a result, retail stocks may suffer. Inflation could be a problem, which would have an impact on the bond market. And so on.

How can you ignore that? Considering all the time people spend analyzing the money supply—a difficult art, at best—it seems to me that some time spent on the weather, which can have a much more pronounced effect on things, is a good idea.

I always carry around a weather forecast in my head. How important do I think that is? The last time I went to Ireland to play golf, I was walking down the fairway of the third hole at Royal Dublin. While waiting my turn, I noticed a caterpillar crawling alongside my ball. Since it was September, I said to my Irish caddy, "You know, he looks like he's got a lot of fur on this year. Does he?" And the caddy said, "Aye. Rough winter ahead."

It was.

IMAGINATION CAN
BE DANGEROUS.

We've all done it. Convinced that ABC Widget Corporation is our big ticket, the one that will, in one fell swoop, bring us home, we pull up the chart.

Examining the chart, we observe the stock's past trading history. Whether that history is up or down, we want to read into it all of our hopes and dreams, so we fill in the chart. We imagine that we see a setup in the chart for higher prices ahead. If the stock has been languishing near a low, we don't imagine a breakdown to new lower lows. Instead, we see a sudden rebound and a new bull trend. If the stock has been rising for the past year, we don't imagine a plunging reversal. Instead, we see a continuation of that bullish trend to new all-time highs. Flag formations are bullish, rectangles are bullish, and support lines are bullish.

Just because we imagine the chart filling with day after day of profitable price action doesn't mean that it will happen. Just because we wish it to be so doesn't mean it will be. The stock will move by its own lights and will wend its own mysterious way to its own conclusion.

Because our minds are wonderfully creative, we can imagine all sorts of conclusions to our adventure in ABC Widgets. Never forget this very human tendency to fill in the chart with what we want to see. Perhaps it will encourage you to spend less time examining the chart and more time examining the company.

SEEK CONFIRMATION.

Watch out if the averages are making new highs while the advance/decline (A/D) line is not improving. The advance/decline line is simply a summation of the number of advancing stocks on a particular exchange or index, versus the number of falling stocks. So, if the advance/decline line on the Dow Industrials is two, it means that 16 stocks were up and 14 down on the day.

The A/D line is a shorthand way of viewing the market, not by an index move but by the plurality of the move. It's as though each stock casts its vote every day about the movement of the market.

When a market advance is a good one, a healthy one, more and more stocks join in. You want to see the vast majority of issues moving higher in a bull move. After all, if you're going to buy a stock, and 80 percent of all stocks are moving higher, the odds are certainly in your favor. Contrast that with a market in which 60 percent of all stocks are moving lower. It's tougher to pick a winner!

While it may seem odd that a market can advance without most stocks participating, just keep in mind that in most indexes, high-priced stocks have a disproportionate effect on the index average, so these big stocks can mask the true movement of the market.

Barron's publishes the A/D line of the New York Stock Exchange every weekend. I always glance at it. I want it moving in the same direction as the market, to confirm the move. When it begins to move in the opposite direction, I begin to question whether or not a turn in the market is at hand. Beware! While the A/D line rarely steers you wrong, it can lag the market for some period of time And it's a slow-moving thing, so don't jump at every little wiggle and move.

BUCKING A TREND
IS A HIGH-RISK GAME.

Proper trading technique means that you trade with the trend. Attempting to trade against the trend means that you are attempting to pick off a top or a bottom, which is really impossible to do over a sustained period of time. Once in a while you can get lucky, but luck is hardly the way to run a successful trading system.

When you trade in the direction of the trend, you tremendously increase your odds of being correct. The market is moving in your direction. Therefore, the odds of buying in at the top or selling at the bottom are about the same as trying to pick off a top or a bottom—very low. If the investment has been rising, then you are a buyer. Conversely, you should be a seller on a falling trend.

If you attempt to use a contratrend system or indicator, you should know that these indicators are notorious for sending false signals. As a matter of fact, many of them fail as much as 50 percent of the time. Whether it's stochastics, Bollinger Bands, Williams %R, or any number of similar constructs, failure rates dictate high levels of caution.

Once in a while you can pick off a top or bottom, which makes you feel that contratrend trading is the only way to go. It is exhilarating when you're right. But never forget that the odds are not in your favor.

CHOOSE SIDES.

You need to decide if you're going to work with trends or against them. This is a basic decision that all investors need to consider and settle. On every entry and exit point, this question is the one that needs to be answered over and over again: Are you investing with the trend or against the trend?

Sometimes you can do both. When selling options, I sometimes sell calls at the top of a trading range and sell puts at the bottom. On another security, I may sell puts in reaction to what I consider to be a primary bull trend. But whatever my decision, I have to have a point of view on the trend in order to work.

For most investors, choosing either one or the other strategy is the best way to proceed. It can be difficult to flip-flop back and forth, depending on the investment. What's more, if you decide, for instance, that you're always going to invest with the trend, then it is easier to develop your system because you practice the same thing, over and over.

I have found that some investors are natural trend followers, while others are more comfortable fading, or trading against, the trend. Just remember the previous advice: Bucking the trend can be a difficult way to go, so choose carefully.

Whatever you choose, be sure you are clear on your basic point of view. It will greatly ease your decision-making process.

POLITICS COUNT.

On average, stocks earn 6 percent a year in the first two years of a presidential administration and 13 percent plus in the final two years.

Simple politics can dictate a market strategy. After a presidential election, politicians, safe from the wrath of the electorate for two to six years, generally embark on the tougher decisions: tax increases, budget decreases, and so forth.

As a result, the first two years of a presidential administration have generally been worse times to invest than the final two years, when things are dressed up for new elections.

It makes sense to be aware of where you are in the presidential cycle, even as you use other market-sensitive indicators.

ALL INDICATORS ARE
NOT EQUAL—BEWARE OF
MISLEADING SIGNALS.

Many investors believe that if open interest on calls or puts is rising, it is a signal that a trend may be changing.

For instance, a sharply rising call open interest would indicate increased bullishness on the part of investors evidenced by their buying more and more call contracts. A quick look tells us that this may be misleading and shouldn't be acted upon.

Open interest in an option contract can be created in one of two ways: First, an investor buys a call contract and that contract is created by the market maker who opens the contract by selling it to the investor. In this case, one contract of open interest is created. Contrarian followers of open interest believe that this action (selling by the knowledgeable market maker and buying by the public) is a bearish indicator.

If only it were that simple!

That same open interest can also be created by an institution (or an individual) selling call contracts against long stock that it holds. That is, the institution believes the stock has limited upside potential (a neutral/bearish point of view), but would rather hold the stock than sell, and is merely trying to increase income by selling option premium. In this case, a new contract is created when the market maker buys the contract from the seller.

But wait! If the market maker buys the contract, isn't that bullish? Isn't this confusing?

Actually, on a day-to-day basis, most options contracts involve investors buying and selling with little change in open interest, which is why open interest can be misleading. You really don't know the motives of the sellers, and you don't know if it is bullish or bearish pressure creating that open interest.

I pay more attention to the number of calls and puts outstanding (the put/call ratio) than I do the number of open contracts. Certainly, it is true that a rising stock will create greater open interest from the buying public who are speculating on a rise in the stock. But, in most cases, it's just not enough to act upon.

DON'T TRUST
VERTICAL MOVES.

From time to time, you'll see something make a vertical move. It may be a stock that rockets from $25 to $60 in two days, or it may be a commodity that increases 25 percent in a week. As a rule, you should stand aside, neither buying nor selling them.

It's easy to spot a vertical move. Just look at the daily chart. Vertical moves reflect an almost complete lack of sellers and a large number of buyers, all eager to get in. The huge imbalance of buyers means that sellers simply mark up the price before letting go.

From a contrarian perspective, vertical moves are minibubbles. In a bubble, there is a similar set of circumstances: Unanimous or near unanimous opinion leads to sharp vertical moves in asset pricing. The difficulty investors have in attempting to trade a vertical move is the same as in attempting to profit in a bubble: Large upward moves are usually followed by similarly large corrections. Another difficulty encountered is that rapid profits, seemingly without effort, energize investors. People have a natural inclination to pile in and perpetuate the move.

In order to put the vertical move in proper perspective, think of it this way: A vertical move creates an increase in risk. If a stock typically trades in a $1 or $2 range per day, it carries a certain amount of inherent volatility. If that range expands to $5 or $10 per day, then in order to invest, you would need to reduce your risk proportionally. So, if you normally buy a 4 percent position in each stock, you might invest 1 percent in a vertical move. You will have roughly the same kind of risk as in buying a normal position. But if you buy a 4 percent position in a stock in a vertical move, you might actually be increasing your risk by a factor of four.

Recognize that a fairly large number of vertical moves are at least partially retraced, so buying into one generally is not a good idea. Better to wait for the retracement (have patience!) to settle the investment down and then enter.

Finally, it is not a good idea to short a vertical move. While you have a good chance of making a profit by doing so, you also run the not unlikely risk that the move will continue, meaning that you haven't picked off the peak.

I usually ignore vertical moves. While they often point the direction for the future, actually trading into one can be dangerous.

IT NEVER RAINS,
BUT IT POURS.

Companies that disappoint Wall Street with earnings announcements are often likely to do so again. If you're an avid consumer of business news, you'll see this play out time and again. A company warns of an earnings shortfall, and the stock takes a hit. Frequently, this isn't a one-time event: Large-magnitude problems usually aren't easily resolved, at least not in time to rebound for the next quarter.

Companies miss earnings estimates for many reasons. Earnings estimates crafted by analysts are sometimes way too high. Perhaps analysts have become too optimistic.

Sometimes, outside events will create problems that are beyond a company's control. For instance, a major earthquake in Taiwan in 1999 damaged many of the semiconductor factories that churned out the silicon chips essential for making PCs. That meant that some American computer manufacturers were going to be short parts. Several manufacturers said that they weren't going to be able to meet production targets and that earnings would fall short as a result.

Other times, the problems are within the company's control. Perhaps the company becomes disorganized and sales falter. Sometimes costs rise out of control or the company doesn't keep up with technology or doesn't develop it further.

These and similar mistakes can result in lower profits, disappointing Wall Street. Worse, these problems typically take time to fix. For investors, the rocket ride is over. Value and contrarian investors may or may not move in, but fast action is gone.

A RISING TIDE
LIFTS ALL BOATS.

Three-quarters of all stocks rise in a bull market; nine-tenths of all stocks fall in a bear market.

It is very difficult to make money if your strategy is contrary to the major trend of the market. It's like trying to fight your way upstream in a small canoe swamped by raging rapids.

When the stock market is rising, most stocks go along for the ride. Good, bad, indifferent, most have been sold down far beyond reasonable value, so a readjustment occurs. In a bear market, the readjustment goes the opposite way. Rampant optimism has pushed most stocks beyond their reasonable value, and the market adjusts quickly to this fact.

What happens is that investors, accustomed to making money in a bull market, continue to buy stocks all the way down to the bottom. They've failed to note that a change in the trend of the market will often override any fundamental in a particular stock. People are often dumbfounded when a stock drops, even after it has dropped a whole lot. They shouldn't be. The major trend of the market is dictating stock prices.

You need to remember a simple fact. In a rising stock market, most stocks go up in price, so the wonders of a bull market will turn a lot of stocks into winners. Some will be deserving and some not, but most will be winners. In a bad market, even the good ones go down.

Postscript

So there you have it. If you've stayed with it this far, I hope you have learned some new things, and found strategies and advice that can help improve your investment returns. I hope somewhere along the way, you have discovered some things that you've done wrong and, perhaps, found the way to correct those mistakes.

To me, it is clear that improving investment technique doesn't come in a series of giant leaps. It is more a matter of slowly getting better, of making those adjustments all the time that add up to something big in the end.

You need patience, and perseverance, and determination to succeed. Investing, after all, is probably among the most competitive of human endeavors. Competition is ferocious and fierce, and all of your emotions are brought into play and conspire to push you off your plan.

Sometimes, it is a wonder to me that people can make any money at all, given the wide and deep array of pitfalls and difficulties in the way. Yet they do, and I think that is a tribute to both the determination that people bring to the problem and the great strength of our capitalist system.

In the end, you will find that investment success is not about picking stocks, or divining interest rates, or setting stop-loss orders. No. In the end, investing is all about mastering yourself. It's about controlling your fear and greed. It involves striving for humility when you win, and acting with grace when you lose. These are the true signposts to which you must turn.

I hope that this book has helped you along the way. Whether improving life for you and your family, or helping you perform your work for your employer, I believe that these pages have offered something that will help you along the path.

Work hard and learn all you can. And don't forget while you're doing that to always control your risk.

INDEX